Metaphor

Metaphor

Denis Donoghue

Harvard University Press
Cambridge, Massachusetts
London, England
2014

Library of Congress Cataloging-in-Publication Data
Donoghue, Denis.
   Metaphor / Denis Donoghue.
      page   cm.
   Includes bibliographical references and index.
   ISBN 978-0-674-43066-2 (alk. paper)
   1. Metaphor—History.   2. Metaphor in literature.
I. Title.

    P301.5.M48D66 2014
    808'.032—dc23   2013037066

To Frances, again

Contents

Introduction   1

Figure   13

After Aristotle   52

No Resemblance   92

"It Ensures That Nothing
   Goes without a Name"   118

Not Quite against Metaphor   143

The Motive for Metaphor   182

Notes   211
Acknowledgments   227
Index   229

Let us begin then with the commonest and by far the most beautiful of tropes, namely *translatio,* which is called *metaphora* in Greek.

—Quintilian, *Institutio Oratoriae,* Book 8.6

Introduction

a metaphor, according to I. A. Richards, is "a shift, a carrying over of a word from its normal use to a new use."[1] That definition is good enough: the root meaning is to transfer a word from one place to another: μεταφερειν. It supposes that there is an ordinary word that could have been used but hasn't been: instead, another word is used that drives the statement in an unexpected direction. Richards calls the ordinary or expected word the *tenor*—whether it's spoken or not—and the unexpected one the *vehicle*. The metaphor is the whole episode, tenor and vehicle together, the relation between the two. Brutus's soliloquy in Shakespeare's *Julius Caesar:*

> Since Cassius first did whet me against Caesar
> I have not slept. (II.1.41–42)

"Whet" is the vehicle; its normal use is to sharpen a knife, a dagger, a sword, or a scythe. Here it displaces literal verbs that might have been used, such as "set me against" or "tempt me." One of these, or something just as literal, would have been used if the decencies of conversation had been in force. The tenor is not spoken, but some such verb is implied. "Whet" also keeps before the audience the motif of stabbing. Eliot writes in "The Waste Land":

> A woman drew her long black hair out tight
> And fiddled whisper music on those strings[2]

The first line is literal, the second metaphorical: the whole metaphor begins with some such unspoken word as "brushed," which would be the tenor. Then the vehicle begins with "fiddled." The point of the metaphor is to bring different associations, more dramatic connotations, into the reader's mind. The resemblance between a woman combing her hair and a violinist with long black hair playing a pianissimo passage is remote—a brush is not much like a bow—but the visual relation is sufficiently active to hold the two images together. If the lines make us imagine for the moment a different world than our own, all the better. The force of a good metaphor is to give something a different life, a new life. A metaphor is all the better the more the vehicle differs from the tenor: it would be a simile if it consorted with the tenor in a local degree of likeness; it would be a conceit if the unlikeness were wild, bizarre, too much of a good thing. A noun, say, by itself, is merely what it is. It is locked in its local meaning, whatever its context deems that to be: a woman is brushing her hair. The effect of Eliot's metaphor is to give her a new, strange life, not by deleting the old one but by drawing a new image across it, that of a woman with long, black hair playing the fiddle. The woman has been given another life for the time being. So have I, when I read it.

In the fourth act of Shakespeare's *Antony and Cleopatra* Antony, defeated at the battle of Actium, betrayed by Cleopatra, cries out in rage and resentment. The people who once fawned on him, licking his sandals, slavering over him, now grovel before the victor, Octavius Caesar. Antony might have said that, but he didn't. He said:

> All come to this? The hearts
> That spanieled me at heels, to whom I gave
> Their wishes, do discandy, melt their sweets
> On blossoming Caesar; and this pine is barked
> That overtopped them all. (IV.xii.20–23)

Five metaphors, explicit or implied. "Spanieled": a transitive verb made from spaniel, a dog commonly thought to be servile, ingratiating, following his master, licking his boots. "Discandy": "to melt or dissolve out of a candied condition," the Oxford English Dictionary (OED) has it, as we would say, sucking a lollipop. The dictionary calls it rare and obsolete and gives only two uses of it, both from *Antony and Cleopatra*. "Melt": to reduce to a liquid state by heat. "On blossoming Caesar": who doesn't need sweets, he's already in blossom. "Is barked": stripped of its bark, left naked to die.

Two metaphors from Tourneur's—if it is his—*The Revenger's Tragedy*. Vindice, bringing on stage a skull got up as a woman:

> Here's an eye
> Able to tempt a great man—to serve God;
> A pretty hanging lip, that has forgot now to dissemble:
> Methinks this mouth should make a swearer tremble,

A drunkard clasp his teeth, and not undo 'em

To suffer wet damnation to run through 'em. (III.v.54–59)

"Wet damnation": drink, but also any further poison a drunk would take into his mouth. "Damnation" is unexpected as the noun after "wet"; it's carried over from a different level of diction. Later, Vindice relishes the thought of killing the nobles at a masque:

Then, ent'ring first, observing the true form,

Within a strain or two we shall find leisure

To steal our swords out handsomely,

And when they think their pleasure sweet and good,

In midst of all their joys, they shall sigh blood. (V.iii.18–22)[3]

There are precedents, though not many, for using "sigh" as a transitive verb, but to sigh blood is unusual: the metaphor makes you see blood pouring out of every victim's mouth as a grotesque sigh, his last. Shakespeare liked to play with different levels of diction. The chorus in his *Henry V*:

Now all the youth of England are on fire,

And silken dalliance in the wardrobe lies: (II. Prologue. 1–2)

"Dalliance" didn't necessarily mean amorous frivolity; it could have that meaning, as in Ophelia's warning to Laertes about the primrose path of dalliance, but it could mean light-hearted talk about anything. "Silken" throws it into high-born idleness, luxurious foreplay. The abstract noun gathers together all the instances, no differentiation being allowed. The adjective, along with "wardrobe," removes doubt.

In "Route 110" Seamus Heaney imagines or recalls going into a second-hand bookstall in Smithfield, Belfast, and buying a used copy of the *Aeneid,* Book 6. The shop assistant, "In a stained front-buttoned shopcoat," emerges from the Classics bay, wondering what to charge, her right hand at work "In the slack marsupial vent / Of her change-pocket."[4] "Marsupial" replaces some other adjective, literal as we say, that would have kept the woman's hand deep in her "shopcoat." My aunt Ciss seemed to spend her life in such a coat, coming out into the shop her broken-down family tried to run on the rare occasions of a customer coming in, and the pouch in the front of it hung loose because of the odds-and-ends it held—small change, a pencil, her reading glasses. I never thought of it as marsupial or of Aunt Ciss as leaping about, a kangaroo in the savannah. Heaney did, seeing the woman in Smithfield as having another life, natural rather than cultural, free rather than constrained; better that than nothing.

In Psalm 118 the psalmist declares that he has enemies and that he will destroy them: "They compassed me about like bees; they are quenched as the fire of thorns: for in the name of the Lord I will destroy them."

"Like bees" is a simile; it is held separate from the "they" it describes. "As the fire of thorns" is a metaphor because it appropri-ates the "they," takes full possession of them, uses them up, con-verts them into a blaze of thorns.

Someone must have invented the first metaphor. J. Hillis Miller thinks he knows who it was: "Surely we have today, after so many generations, gone beyond the naiveté of Rousseau's prim-itive man who, in his first encounter with another man, out of fear called him a giant and so invented the first metaphor, the archetrope on the ground of which all the airy fabric of language has been constructed, in an endless series of displacements from that first erroneous figure?"[5]

I imagine a more somber figure looking at something, think-ing of the standard word for it in her native language, and feeling sad that the thing is merely what it is; it has no other life. She might then have invented a simile, thinking that the thing was like something else, but that wouldn't be enough. It wouldn't alter the first thing substantially; it would just give it a notional, provisional quality, limited to obvious likeness. She might then feel impelled to go further and give it another life, perhaps a better one. It would be a daring gesture, flouting the authority by which the first thing stays as it is. She would imagine some other thing that the first thing might have been or might still be, in an alternative world. And aeons and aeons later a man called Job would cry out, "I am a brother to dragons, and a companion to owls" (Job 30:29). Two metaphors. As James Wood has said, more than once, but this once about V. S. Pritchett: Like Shakespeare and Dickens, he saw that the metaphorical is central to writing, and central to character; that characters expand via metaphor—they are, as the word suggests, carried over, changed into something else in the process of using metaphor—and that readers expand metaphorically when they encounter metaphor. It can and should be said of Pritchett that he secures the Englishness of metaphor while carrying it over into something forever un-English, forever changed.[6]

He means Chekhov.

Richards's definition isn't sharp enough to distinguish metaphor from other nearby figures. In the first scene of Shakespeare's *Hamlet* Horatio might have said to Marcellus, "Look! It is the dawn!" but he didn't, he said:

> But, look, the morn, in russet mantle clad,
> Walks o'er the dew of yon high eastward hill (I.1.167–168)

I would call this a personification, not a metaphor: "in russet mantle," "clad," and "walks" speak of an inanimate thing as if it were human. Sometimes it is hard to distinguish personification from metaphor, but in this instance Horatio's exclamation has more attributes of one than the other. Eliot quotes the lines, more than once, in "Poetry and Drama," without naming the figure they make:

> When we hear the lines—
>> But, look, the morn, in russet mantle clad,
>> Walks o'er the dew of yon hid eastern [eastward] hill,
> we are lifted for a moment beyond character, but with no sense of unfitness of the words coming, and at this moment, from the lips of Horatio. The transitions in the scene obey laws of the music of dramatic poetry.[7]

But he had already, one page back, noted the anticipation of the plot in Horatio to the ghost, "What art thou that usurp'st this time of night?"

To say that something is something else and to force you to think of it in that new way—which is the practice of metaphor—rarely has large consequence, except to yourself, but sometimes it has. On June 25, 2012, the U.S. Supreme Court refused to reconsider its decision of 2010 that outside spending by corporations in election campaigns is a constitutional right guaranteed by the First Amendment protecting free speech. To reach that decision, the court had to say, as *Buckley v. Valeo* did in 1976, that the expenditure of money in election campaigns is a form of speech. To declare that money is speech is to activate the metaphorical capacity of the English language. The consequences of this declaration have already been immense in the conduct of the 2012 presidential election. The book that follows is a study of metaphor in a quieter setting.

Normally, there is a single tenor, saying what the subject is, the thing we're talking about. The vehicle is also single, the new thing we want someone to think of while officially thinking about the tenor. If the vehicle speaks of more than one thing at a time, we have a mixed metaphor, unless the two or more things are close kin. The five metaphors from *Antony and Cleopatra* are not mixed, they are serial, one then another then another to a count of five. In a mixed metaphor, the vehicle is impacted and we have to think—or try to—of the two or more together. If I say that "Sally is a block of ice," there is no problem; the metaphor says (roughly) that she is frigid, emotionally cold. If I say, redundantly, that "Sally is a block of ice, hard to thaw," there is still no problem, the metaphor is intact. But if I say that "Sally is a block of ice, hard to remove," the metaphor is mixed. A certain metaphorical claim begins with "a block of ice," but "remove" enforces a literal statement by reaching back to a standard object for that verb, namely "block," some obstacle to be removed. The mixture of metaphor and literal statement catches us in a quandary; we don't know which way to turn. Mixed metaphors are said to be bad, because they confuse our minds, one vehicle crashing into another; instead of giving us a glorious future, they hold us in a frustrated present.

But there are doubtful cases. I'll mention two. Shakespeare's Lady Macbeth, scorning her husband's inclination to back off from the planned murder of Duncan—"We will proceed no further in this business"—says:

> Was the hope drunk
> Wherein you dress'd yourself? Hath it slept since?
> And wakes it now, to look so green and pale
> At what it did so freely? (*Macbeth*, I.vii.35–38)

Cleanth Brooks has emphasized the many references to clothes and drink in the play, but the one I've quoted seems to me the most exacting of the lot. The hope is the plan we made to kill Duncan. Were you drunk when we made it? The awkward word is "dress'd." The other words denote a drunk waking up liverish with a hangover. Was he already drunk when he put on his trousers and strutted into talk of murder? "Dress'd" mixes the metaphor up. But it doesn't do any harm; Lady Macbeth is talking hard and strong, but measured statement is not an issue.

The second case needs more elucidation. Henry James published *Roderick Hudson* in twelve installments of the *Atlantic Monthly* in 1875. The book appeared at the end of the year and was reviewed anonymously in *The Nation* on March 9, 1876. In fact, the reviewer was James's friend Grace Norton, Charles Eliot Norton's sister. The review was witty and well-intentioned, but its negative sentences were more memorable than its words of praise. Of Roderick and Rowland, the reviewer said: "The anomalous relation of these two young men, who are sometimes comrades on the footing of good fellowship, and sometimes separated into a modest and most conscientious and responsible patron and a ward now wholly self-surrendering and endearing and again obstinately resisting and repelling, is so strange a flaw in the story as to damage it throughout."[8]

Shortly after the review appeared, Grace Norton wrote to Henry James to acknowledge that she had written it. I have not seen her letter, so I have to deduce its tendency from James's reply, dated March 31. It appears that Grace Norton took the occasion to include some further criticisms that the editor of *The Nation* had cut out. If her tone was apologetic, on the whole, James insisted that the apology was unnecessary; he protested that he liked the review; it was "extremely kindly, graceful, neatly turned, felicitous—everything that a review should be": "Behold me then healed of wounds I have never felt, wiping away tears I have never shed, all because in this world it is well to take all one can get & if reparation isn't à propos now it is very well to lay in a stock of it in view of future contingencies." James agreed that some of the words and phrases that Grace Norton had reflected on were indeed errors, but he defended one metaphor although he conceded that it was "indeed a trifle mixed." In Chapter 9 Rowland Mallet is in Rome, and he goes to St. Peter's, where he meets Madame Grandoni. She tells him that "Christina Light was married this morning to Prince Casamassima." Mallet is appalled. In the conversation that follows he speculates that Christina's marriage to the prince, whom she is known to detest, can be accounted for only by her dread that her illegitimacy might be revealed. Madame Grandoni says, "Christina was forced to decide, then, that she could not afford not to be a princess." Mallet's theory about illegitimacy might be nonsense, as Madame Grandoni exclaims, but not, he says, "to the proudest girl in the world, deeply wounded in her pride, and not stopping to calculate probabilities, but muffling her shame, with an almost sensuous relief, in a splendor that stood within her grasp and asked no questions."[9] Grace Norton must have scolded James for the mixed metaphor, going wild with "splendor." He replied, "Lastly, the metaphor about muffling shame in a splendor that asks no questions is indeed a trifle mixed; but it is essentially a loose metaphor—it isn't a simile—it doesn't pretend to sail close to the wind. Still, it is certainly very happy that that splendor does ask no questions: the fewer the better."[10]

"Calculate probabilities": including the probability that her illegitimacy will be found out anyway. "Muffling her shame": as in

OED, "to wrap or cover up or enfold, especially so as to conceal."
Muffling her shame is metaphorical, but the problem begins with
"a splendor," which is no longer a free-standing abstraction; the
little "a" makes it personal to her. "A splendor that stood within
her grasp and asked no questions" is really a personification,
emphasized by the human verbs "stood" and "asked." It is not
clear what James means by claiming that "it is essentially a loose
metaphor—it isn't a simile—it doesn't pretend to sail close to the
wind." I think he means that a simile says that one thing is like
another, no equivocation permitted. A simile about her shame
would have made Mallet shameless. A secure metaphor would
have lodged her shame in a far richer cluster of sensations, but
with the risk of making the whole become dangerous: you never
know what fragment of news will split off from the main body
and do all the harm in the world. James took Grace Norton's observation seriously, to the extent of resorting to another figure to
disarm it. This last one is a figure of danger risked and just barely
avoided, and the only danger mentioned is that of making a simile; but a simile between what constituents? It could only have
been a simile comparing "a splendor" to something else, presumably some version of the figure standing within Christina's grasp
and asking no questions. James was keen to hold on to the metaphor, loose or strict. In the English edition of 1879 he changed
the sentence that bothered Grace Norton to read "a splendor that
stood within her grasp and would cover everything." This tones
down the personification, replacing the personal verb "asked" by
the impersonal "covered." The metaphor is not as loose as it was,
but it is still mixed. James was sanguine about such things; he was
careful to get his sentences right, but when he got one wrong, he
wasn't distressed to be found out. I hope my dragging it in and

commenting on it so long hasn't worn your patience beyond thinness.

My first chapter is irrepressibly autobiographical; it insisted. The middle chapters are better behaved, their themes more-or-less self-evident. In "It Ensures That Nothing Goes without a Name," I take up again some of the issues looked at in earlier chapters but now in a wider or at least a different context. In "Not Quite against Metaphor" I consider some of the honorable reasons why one might keep one's distance from metaphor, or disapprove of the glamor that surrounds it. I hope these considerations will not be found decisive.

Figure

The word figure is itself obviously metaphorical.

—Paul Ricoeur

*f*igures of speech, figures of thought: I was suffused with metaphors and other figures before I knew there were such things. When I was a boy, growing up in Warrenpoint, County Down, Northern Ireland, from about 1932 to 1942, I attended evening devotions with my mother at our local Catholic Church, St. Peter's. My father and my brother Tim accompanied us to Mass on Sundays, but they did not extend their observance beyond that duty. My father was a straightforward Catholic, but he was not devout. Tim was sullen as if on principle, but even in his most truculent moods he did not refuse to go to Mass. My sisters May and Kathleen attended boarding school in Newry, five miles away, so their religious practice was under the care of the nuns of the Convent of Mercy. Regularly, at evening benediction, my mother and I recited with the priest and the congregation the Litany of the Blessed Virgin Mary:

Tower of ivory,

House of gold,

Ark of the Covenant,

Gate of Heaven,

Morning star . . .

Nobody told me that these phrases were metaphors or explained
what they had to do with the Blessed Virgin. I felt no inclination to ask; their holy sounds were enough. It was sufficient that
my voice blended with the general voice of the congregation. In
A Portrait of the Artist as a Young Man Mrs. Riordan doesn't want
Stephen Dedalus to play with Eileen "because Eileen was a
Protestant and when she was young she knew children that used
to play with Protestants and the Protestants used to make fun of
the litany of the Blessed Virgin": "*Tower of Ivory,* they used to say,
House of Gold! How could a woman be a tower of ivory or a house
of gold?"[1]

Like me, Stephen had never heard of metaphor, but he resolved
the question to his gratification by staring at Eileen's hands: "Eileen had long white hands. One evening when playing tig she had
put her hands over her eyes: long and white and thin and cold and
soft. That was ivory: a cold white thing. That was the meaning of
Tower of Ivory."[2]

He did not question the propriety of attaching that meaning—a
cold white thing—to the Blessed Virgin. When he watches Eileen
running down "the sloping curve of the path," he thinks of further associations: "Her fair hair had streamed out behind her like
gold in the sun. *Tower of Ivory. House of Gold.* By thinking of things
you could understand them."[3] Not necessarily: by thinking of
things you could also get them wrong. I often took things for

Figure   15

granted, having no Eileen to play tig with or to yearn for, in five slow adjectives, appreciatively spaced by and and and and and. Stephen was content to let one image of gold tell him of another.

I was an altar boy at St. Peter's, serving at Mass for Father Mc-Mullan or Canon (as he then was) McAlister. On Sundays, if I was not serving, I sang in the choir. Mass was in Latin, and so were the hymns. Hymns in English were permitted on minor occasions—I recall "I'll Sing a Hymn to Mary" and "Nearer my God to Thee"—but not at Mass. The hymns that have stayed most insistently in my head since those days are "Adoro te devote," "Panis angelicus," "Ave verum corpus natum," and "Pange lingua." I remember, more remotely, "Lauda, Sion, salvatorem," and "Vexilla Regis." At benediction we sang "O Salutaris hostia" and the part of "Pange lingua" that begins: "Tantum ergo sacramentum." At stations of the cross we sang, very slowly, "Stabat mater dolorosa," though the themes we were called upon to meditate were announced in English. The hymn was like carrying the cross: I thought the burden of it would never end and that I could not survive till it did. I don't think we were required to attempt the dreadful eloquence of "Dies irae."

I was a boy soprano—my voice had not yet broken—and I sang solo every few Sundays. My favorite hymn as a soloist was "Panis angelicus," accompanied by Seán Crawford on the organ. The words (as I later learned) were by St. Thomas Aquinas, the music by César Franck. I knew only as much Latin as I could pick up, dropped from those hymns and the Latin of the Mass. It was easy to sing the Latin hymns because you could pronounce the words—the syllables, rather—as if they were English. My mother, with little formal education, had no difficulty speaking the Latin responses at Mass. That would not have been possible if the official language of the church were Greek or Jesus's Aramaic. Not that my mother and I needed to know even the rudiments of church Latin. We were guided sufficiently to the sacraments and rituals by the images that filled the spaces, walls, and stained-glass windows of St. Peter's—the altar, the holy water font, the stations of the cross, the Blessed Virgin, and the Pietà came together to make ecstatic resonance: that was enough. I had not yet heard of rhyme and assonance, but I'm sure I felt some congruence of sound between the "angelicus" of the first line of "Panis angelicus" and the "coelicus" a few lines later, though one had four syllables and the other three. I sang them as if that were devoutly to be recognized.[4]

I did not begin to learn Latin till I left the school in Warrenpoint and started attending the Christian Brothers' School in Newry. Latin, taught by Mr. Crinion, soon became my favorite subject. We made our way happily through the *Christian Brothers' Latin Grammar,* some of Cicero's letters and speeches, selected passages of the *Aeneid,* and the easiest of Horace's odes. I loved Latin, the foreignness of it. Later, when I went to University College, Dublin, I continued my study of Latin—a major subject leading to an honors degree in arts (as we called the humanities). Dr. John O'Meara guided us through the niceties of Latin poetry and versification, Professor Patrick Semple had us translate passages of Tacitus, aloud.

Many years passed before I thought of Aquinas's Latin hymns, but now they keep coming to me without invitation. When I think of my childhood in Warrenpoint, I hear "Panis angelicus" at the back of my mind, crossed with the pity of "Stabat mater." I have only recently asked myself what Aquinas said in those hymns. In Warrenpoint I sang the syllables, which I stroked—I see now—as my boyish taste required: the words and their meanings had to fend for themselves. In fact, the question of their meanings never occurred to me, and I lived agreeably enough without it: what-

Figure 17

ever the relation was between "angelicus" and "coelicus," I could let it rest in its halo of sanctity. Latin to me was an experience like those of smelling incense and striking the gong. Serving at Mass, I was in charge of the gong. At appropriate moments I struck it, let it sound for a few seconds, then stilled it by clasping it with my left hand. It was up to me to decide how long the echo should last. The duration was exquisite. At benediction I lifted the thurible—as we called the censer—with my right hand and the silver boat of incense with my left. Father McMullan then took a small spoonful of incense and poured it slowly on the smoking charcoal. The smell of sanctity was thrilling. I wanted it never to end. Father McMullan swung the thurible slowly, and the smoke and the smell drifted through the church. It was my introduction to luxury. Latin, the gong, and incense were promises of happiness, even though I didn't know what they meant. Now I find that, even with my somewhat stronger Latin, I hardly know what I was singing. The smell of incense is still to me an unquestioned joy. I hardly need to learn from the book of Revelation (5:8) that the golden bowls full of incense are "the prayers of saints." It was pure pleasure to be immersed in those sensations. My relation to Catholicism was one of total immersion without fuss or fret. Faith and my sensory experience were one and the same. I was not troubled by the magnificence of Father McMullan's surplice. When Aunt Ciss crocheted a deep round of crucifixes to adorn my own surplice, I thought it a fine possession. Even the practice of going to confession every Saturday evening held no fears, since I did not commit any sins. I had to pretend to a few peccadilloes to make it reasonable to go at all.

I have consulted Father Walter J. Ong's essay, "Wit and Mystery: A Revaluation in Mediaeval Latin Hymnody," and some other aids to get my bearings on Aquinas's hymns.[5] What I have mainly learned is that they are so rampant with wordplay, puns, and conceits that I could not have understood them in Warrenpoint even if my teacher, Mr. Crawford, had taken me aside and construed them for me word by word. I don't think Mr. Crinion, splendid as he was, could have resolved the theological intricacies of Aquinas's Latin. Father Ong speculated that modern readers would appreciate the poetry of Aquinas's hymns, instructed as they were by T. S. Eliot to refine their sense of poetic language. Eliot's presentation of Donne, Herbert, Marvell, Crashaw, and other metaphysical poets of the seventeenth century brought forth new values in reading poems. Ong referred to "current interests which have resulted in the now matured appreciation of the once disreputable 'metaphysical' poetry of seventeenth-century England."[6] The title of "Wit and Mystery" acknowledges the passage in Eliot's essay on Marvell in which, with the "Horatian Ode," Cowley's Anacreontic poems, and Milton's "Comus" in mind, Eliot wrote of wit as a quality of those poems and described it as "a tough reasonableness beneath the slight lyric grace."[7] Ong didn't quote Eliot's phrase, but he addressed Aquinas's hymns in its light.

The "Pange lingua," for instance, has these lines, as difficult as any in Donne, and enough verbal business to defeat a translator:

> Verbum caro panem verum
> verbo carnem efficit,
> fitque sanguis Christi merum,
> et, si sensus deficit,
> ad firmandum cor sincerum
> sola fides sufficit.[8]

Figure   19

Peter Walsh's translation reads:

> Word-made-flesh transforms the true bread
>   by the word into his flesh;
> wine is changed into the Christ's blood;
>   and, if sense fails to discern,
> faith alone is found sufficient
>   to strengthen devoted hearts.[9]

Even a scholar as resourceful as Father Ong did not offer to translate the hymn into English verse. He commented:

> Thomas is here concerned with the fact that it was not God the Father nor God the Holy Spirit, but the Second Person, God the Word, Who became flesh, and that this same Word, when He wishes to convert bread into His flesh uses *words* as the instruments for His action. This is a coincidence startling enough and too good to be missed, the more so because the use of words in connection with its sacramental ritual was plainly distinctive of the New Law inaugurated after the Word had entered the material world as man: the Paschal Lamb, which in the Old Law prefigured the Eucharistic Sacrifice, had, like most other "sacraments" of the Old Law, no special verbal formula connected with it.[10]

That comment was a help, but it didn't cope with Aquinas's Latin. Hugh Kenner, following Father Ong, tried a different approach:

> The identities in the Latin are so close we cannot tell where to commence translating: *verbum* and *verum* and *carnem* and *panem* are but glimpses of a central reality, word and bread

and flesh and truth, flashing in mutated sounds its multiple aspect. "The word makes flesh made of its flesh, a true bread by a word": so one possible paraphrase might stumble. The poet too makes such miracles happen with a word, bemusing our senses with intertwined words. (By no accident, the Symbolist Movement in France would one day be staffed by lapsed Catholics.) And the "sensus" that is deficient is simultaneously the fivefold sensual extension of man's body, overwhelmed by reality, and the sense that inheres in language, incapable of wholly distinguishing what is indistinguishable, or of effecting the unity of what must be named serially, hence separately. *Efficit,* God brings to pass; *deficit,* man's mind stumbles; and yet *sufficit,* faith makes good. Aquinas, a considerable poet, intends here with the utmost seriousness a virtual transubstantiation of language, untinctured by any need to show off virtuosity.[11]

My own stumbling paraphrase would read: "The Word made flesh turns ordinary bread into his flesh by his word. (Ordinary) wine becomes the blood of Christ; and if (our) sense fails (to apprehend the change), faith alone is enough to strengthen a sincere heart." But that doesn't register the wordplay of "verbum, verum, verbo"; "panem, carnem"; "verum, merum, sincerum; efficit, deficit, sufficit," or the end rhymes, strong punctuation for the ear.

My belated interest in these hymns is the result of two preoccupations: a renewed engagement with figures, tropes, and especially metaphor—and with the neighboring figures, simile, metonymy, catachresis, and synecdoche. I interpret *figure* as the grand term that encompasses these lesser ones. My second, but not secondary,

Figure   21

preoccupation is with problems of reading, not at all resolved by my having published *The Practice of Reading* several years ago. I think of reading as enchanted interpretation that sometimes involves foraging among the available senses of a word or a phrase to settle upon the one that seems most justly telling in its place. Then there is the question of ambiguity—William Empson's concern in *Seven Types of Ambiguity, Some Versions of Pastoral,* and *The Structure of Complex Words*—where an equivocal word may point to psychological trouble in the author or a double meaning come upon in the language and taken up by the writer as a gift of chance. But what makes a particular interpretation seem "most justly telling"? How to read a metaphor—that is the conjunction of these interests, because on the face of it a metaphor—as in "on the face of it"—is bizarre. Why say that something is something else? Hopkins has a poem, "The Blessed Virgin Compared to the Air We Breathe," but he doesn't say that she is, in fact, the air we breathe. Roland Barthes spoke of metaphor "in the banal sense of an image that makes a comparison."[12] Why is that sense banal? What is entailed by comparing one thing to another? Is it true that we live upon resemblances and upon the differences among them? How does a metaphor differ from a simile?

It was encouraging to learn from Father Ong that Aquinas asked himself whether or not theology, if it is a strict science, can be justified in using metaphor, and decided, notably in his commentary on Peter Lombard, that it could: "The science of poetry is about things which because of their deficiency of truth [*propter defectum veritatis*] cannot be laid hold of by reason. Hence reason has to be drawn off to the side by means of certain similitudes [*quibusdam similitudinibus seducatur*]. But then, theology is also about things which lie beyond reason [*supra rationem*]. Thus the

symbolic method [*modus symbolicus*] is common to both, since neither is accommodated [to human reason]."[13]

Aquinas held poetics to be "below the strict logic of scientific
demonstration," as Father Ong mentions, and below dialectic and
rhetoric, but at least he allowed for kinship between metaphor
and theological discourse.[14] In the *Summa* (Ia, qu. 13, art 6) he
asked himself "whether names predicated of God are predicated
primarily of creatures," and he answered that "all names that are
applied metaphorically to God are applied to creatures primarily
rather than to God, because when said of God they mean only
similitudes to such creatures." Raising the question "whether sacred scripture should use metaphors," he answered that "Sacred
Scripture delivers spiritual things to us under metaphors taken
from bodily things."[15] But "the beam of divine revelation is not
extinguished by the sense imagery that veils it; its truth does not
flicker out; because the minds of those to whom the revelation is
given are not allowed to remain arrested by the images but are
lifted up to their meaning."[16] Not that Aquinas worried much
about metaphor for the sake of poetry. He regarded poetry as an
infima scientia, much inferior to philosophy. He wrote poems only
when called upon by the pope to do so, and even then he wrote
them only in respect of the Blessed Sacrament: no other theme
provoked his poetic imagination.

Aquinas wrote "Panis angelicus" for matins of Corpus Christi
and of the Votive Office of the Most Blessed Sacrament, a feast
day instituted by Pope Urban IV in 1264. I first heard it, I must
believe, without really hearing it. My father brought me to Dublin to attend the Thirty-First International Eucharistic Congress,
held in Phoenix Park from June 22 to June 26, 1932. The con-

Figure   23

gress celebrated the 1500th anniversary of St. Patrick's coming to Ireland to convert the natives. I don't know why my father decided to make the trip; he must have been impelled by picturesque rather than religious considerations. No image or sense of the event has remained with me. I don't recall where we lodged or took our meals. I suppose we travelled by train. I know—it is a matter of record—that the great Irish tenor John McCormack sang "Panis angelicus" at the open-air High Mass in the park on June 26, but not a note of the occasion has lodged in my memory. I was three and a half years old at the time, too young to remember much. Why my father brought me with him, I have no idea, except that I was his pet. In Ireland to this day devout Catholics warm to César Franck's setting of the hymn. When McCormack recorded it, Catholics held his performance in far greater esteem than the national anthem or "Faith of Our Fathers." Franck composed the music in 1872 for tenor, harp, cello, and organ, but it is generally sung by a solo tenor or soprano or, as in my case, a boy soprano.

Years later, when I tried to construe Aquinas's Latin in "Panis angelicus," I was brought up sharp by the first lines:

Panis angelicus
fit panis hominum:
dat panis coelicus
figuris terminum.

That is to say: "The angelic bread becomes the bread of man: the heavenly bread puts a stop to figures." What does that mean? Why does Aquinas now welcome the stopping of figures of speech and thought, if that is what the words say?

The first answer I found came from Kenner:

"Dat panis coelicus figuris terminum," wrote Thomas Aquinas. The heavenly nourishment (bread and flesh at once) has put an end to "figures." Figures can only say, "This is 'like' what cannot be shown; what you see is an emblem." No more of that now: no more of *this* making shift to "represent" *that.* We have the gift of the Eucharist, which *is* what it represents. Polyhedral Being is gathered together now, the faces different yet identical.[17]

"Polyhedral": many-sided, many-faced. In some moods I can understand the pleasure of getting rid of figures, the repetitive boredom of eking out *this* by its likeness to *that,* even if you have to qualify the claim by allowing for differences between these constituents. Good riddance may be good enough, or not. It would be a relief, in such a mood, to say and keep on saying: This is itself; it is exactly what it says it is. It coincides with itself. There is no lack in the description, no need to have my mind "drawn off to the side"—another metaphor. But that can't be what Aquinas meant.

The gift of the Eucharist did not, in practice—even in Aquinas's practice—put a stop to figures. Here is the first stanza of "Adoro te devote" in the version we sang in Warrenpoint. The music is the magisterial Gregorian chant:

Adoro te devote, latens deitas,
quae sub his figuris vere latitas;
tibi se cor meum totum subicit,
quia te contemplans totum deficit.

That is to say: "Devotedly I worship You, Deity who are concealed, / under these figures truly lying hid. / My heart subjects itself entirely to you, / for, contemplating you, it wholly faints

Figure   25

away."[18] I gather from Father Ong's essay and from F. J. E. Raby's
History of Christian-Latin Poetry that "deitas" should be replaced by
"veritas." Peter Walsh's text has "formis" for "figuris." Someone,
according to Father Ong, "has piously watered down [Aquinas's]
concept to a different one admitting of a more indiscriminate sort
of response."[19] Aquinas remembered Isaiah 45:15: "Verily thou art
a god that hidest thyself, O God of Israel, the Savior." Aquinas
rhymes the mystery: abstract noun with verb in the second person
singular, "latens veritas" with "vere latitas." "Vere" is a bold challenge, "truly" hidden. I learned from Andrei Gotia that "figurae"
describes the species "of bread and wine, indicating that the first
form of Eucharistic adoration is the Holy Mass, while the Latin
his shows proximity, in heart and space, to the Holy Eucharist."[20]
It seems bizarre that these should be got rid of in "Panis Angelicus," even in deference to the Eucharist, unless they have nothing
to do with speech or thought. The hidden deity puts the figures
in an equivocal posture.

Andrei Gotia sent me to an essay by Robert Wielockx that
presents a somewhat different text of "Adoro te devote" and a
more elaborate reading of it. Wielockx has based his text on a col-
lation of fifty-one witnesses, forty-eight of which are manuscript
copies. The first two lines of his text are:

> Adoro te deuote, latens ueritas,
> te que sub his formis uere latitas.

The replacement of "figuris" by "formis" is obscure to me, unless
"forma" is a more emphatic word for the visible bread and wine.
Wielockx makes a point of referring to Aquinas's "continuous
teaching . . . according to which the senses are not wrong when
they judge their proper object, which, as far as the Eucharist is

concerned, is only the sacramental species."[21] These forms are indeed as the senses see them. "Not only do the senses not err in their perceptions; without this sense perception of the sacramental species, faith and adoration, as the author understands them here, would be impossible."[22] "That Aquinas evidently agrees with the teaching of the pseudo-Dionysus the Areopagite, according to which the Eucharist is not a sacrament like others but the very perfection of the sacramental order, is scarcely surprising."[23] But it leaves the displacement of "figuris" by "formis" obscure. I wonder: could there be a contradiction between Aquinas's use of "figurae" in the two hymns, unless he is being entirely legal in using the word in two different senses? It may be that "figura" and "forma" are synonyms, though they don't sound like synonyms to me.

At that point in my foraging and on Gotia's advice, I appealed for further guidance to Father John Saward, formerly professor of Dogmatic Theology at the International Theological Institute in Gamens, Austria, and asked him: Is Aquinas contradicting himself or is he using the word "figura" in two different senses? Father Saward's reply was so informative that I give it here in full. Not a word of it can be subtracted:

> When St. Thomas says that the Blessed Sacrament "puts an end to figures," he means that the period of prefiguring and foreshadowing (the Old Testament) is at an end. He makes the same point in the *Pange lingua:* "Types and shadows have their ending, for the newer rite is here." The Manna in the Wilderness and the Passover Lamb were both types, prefigurings, of the Eucharist. The "sacraments" of the Old Testament, as both St. Augustine and St. Thomas call the sacred rites of the Jews, were only symbols of a glorious reality still

Figure   27

to come: that reality is Jesus, true God and true man, the true
Bread from Heaven and Lamb of God, who is present in His
very substance under the sacramental species.

Father Saward's letter leads me to the second meaning of "figura," in the "Adoro te: sub his figuris vere latitas." Evidently, here
"figure" is synonymous with "accidents" or "species" or "form"
(in the sense of accidental form). In his first article on the real
presence in the *Summa* (3a, qu. 73, a.1), St. Thomas shows that
the body of Christ is in the blessed sacrament not just "secundum
figuram vel sicut in signo" but "secundum veritatem." The here-
tic Berengarius thought that our Lord was in the blessed sacrament in a merely symbolic, figurative way: for him, the substance
of bread and wine continued to be there after the consecration,
and were just the symbols of the body and the blood, which were
absent. But for St. Thomas, the whole substance of the bread is
changed into the body of Christ, and the whole substance of wine
into his blood, the accidents of bread and wine ("bare shadows,
shape and nothing more," as Hopkins renders St. Thomas) remain after the consecration, but without a subject in which to
inhere.[24] Now these accidents, appearances, can be said to be a
"sign," or even "figure" of the body and blood of Christ in the
sense that they are a sign and figure of the body and blood that *are*
now present—truly, really, and substantially: "In the opening
lines of the *Adoro te* St. Thomas focuses on the presence of the
Divinity of our Lord, but of course the whole Christ—Body,
Blood, Soul, and Divinity—is present in the Blessed Sacrament
under both species."[25] Father Saward's last sentence, about the
"Adoro te," apparently refers to "deitas" rather than "ueritas" in
the first line. The passage in "Pange lingua" that he mentions is:

Tantum ergo sacramentum
veneremur cernui;
et antiquum documentum
novo cedat ritui:
praestet fides supplementum
sensuum defectui.

In Walsh's translation: "We this sacrament of greatness / will revere on bended knee, / and the observance of the ancients, / yield to a new form of rite. / Let faith make its own addition / to our senses' failing powers."[26]

Father Saward's letter, so generous in its clarity, gave me all the bearings I could cope with. It also allowed me to think that *figure,* in Christian hymnody, refers not first and foremost to rhetorical figures but to motifs or images in the Old Testament, which Aquinas and the church fathers interpreted as foreshadowings, prefigurings of the new, and that, after this fulfillment in the Eucharist, figures refer to shadows, accidents, of the sacramental body and blood of Christ. St. Paul writes in 1 Cor. 4:6: "And these things, brethren, I have in a figure transferred to myself and to Apollos for your sake." I don't recall that the first line of "Adoro te" gave me much trouble: the intimacy of "te," followed by the abstraction of "deitas" or "veritas" might be a problem, except that the hiddenness of "divinity" or of "truth" is itself to be adored, because it is a sign of God's uniqueness; if it were not his distinctive mark, the difference between God and man would be cancelled. But I eventually wanted to know how one word, "figure," could do such double duty, and how "figure" and "form" came to be synonyms, if they did. Perhaps they had nothing to do with rhetorical figures. Peter Burian has pointed out to me that a literal

Figure   29

translation of the crucial lines in "Pange Lingua"—"Verbum caro panem verum / verbo carnem efficit"—would seem to reject figure or form entirely by substituting eucharistic identity for mere likeness: "Word–flesh by [his] word makes true bread [into his] flesh." This speaks to the unfiguring of apparently figural language—"figuris terminum." Erich Auerbach's great essay, "Figura," I later learned, was the place to go for instruction.

In rhetoric, according to the OED, figure means "any of the various 'forms' of expression, deviating from the normal arrangement or use of words, which are adopted in order to give beauty, variety, or force to a composition; e.g. Aposiopesis, Hyperbole, Metaphor, etc." (21a). Deviation from common or ordinary usage is emphasized. There is no need to refer to proper or literal speech; usage is sufficient authority. Auerbach's essay and several chapters of *Mimesis* give historical warrant.

The earliest works of Christian literature were written in Greek, and the standard word for "prefiguration" was *typos*. Auerbach reports that the earliest known occurrence of *figura* is in Terence, where it means "plastic form." A young girl in *Eunuchus* has a "nova figura oris," a new form of face. The proper history of the word begins with the Hellenization of Roman education in the last century BC. Varro, Lucretius, and Cicero are the main authorities. Varro uses *figura* to mean "outward appearance" or even "outline." We still say of a girl, improperly: she has a good figure. Clearing up a point of my ignorance, Varro also "uses *figura* and *forma* interchangeably, in the general sense of form."[27] He uses it too as a term in grammar, *figura multitudinis* meaning the form of the plural. *Figura* meant the seal stamped in wax. Lucretius used it "in every possible shading from the plastic figure shaped by man . . . to the purely geometric outline." He was mainly responsible for turning the word toward *simulacra,* the resemblance of children to their parents, and the images delivered by dreams. Atoms, as in the cosmogony of Democritus and Epicurus, were called *figurae.* Cicero used the word in virtually all his contexts—political, juridical, and philosophical; it means semblance as well as a figure of speech, *figura dicendi,* but that particular *figura* only denotes a mode of eloquence. Cicero had perceptible form mainly in mind: "It is in Cicero and the author of the *Ad Herennium* that [the word] occurs for the first time as a technical term in rhetoric, rendering . . . the three levels of style, which in *Ad Herennium* are designated as *figura gravis, mediocris,* and *extenuata* . . . and in *De oratore* as *plena, mediocris,* and *tenuis.*" By the end of the republican era, *figura* was well established in the language of philosophy and cultivated discourse; it was easily available to Catullus, Propertius, and especially Ovid. When the meter called for a dissyllabic word, Ovid used *forma* freely, but he preferred *figura,* and used it in many situations, commonplace and erotic: "Venerem iungunt per mille figuras," they embrace in a thousand positions. In Vitruvius's writings *figura* means an architect's ground plan. Pliny the Elder directed the word toward portrait painting. Sometimes, as in the juridical literature of the first century, *figura* meant "empty outward form" or mere semblance.

But the most far-reaching development of the word in the first century came, according to Auerbach, with the refinement of the concept of the rhetorical figure. Quintilian is the crucial writer here, so much so that Aristotle, Longinus, Cicero, and Quintilian virtually divide the field of rhetoric among them. In the last section of Book 8 and throughout Book 9 of the *Institutio oratoria,* Quintilian gives a detailed account of the theory of tropes and

Figure   31

figures. As Auerbach says, "Trope is the more restricted concept, referring to the use of words and phrases in a sense other than literal; figure, on the other hand, is a form of discourse which deviates from the normal and most obvious usage." Put like that, it is hard to see how one hand differs from the other. Basically, Auerbach reports, "all discourse is a forming, a figure, but the word [*figura*] is employed only for formations that are particularly developed in a poetic or rhetorical sense." Quintilian distinguishes between a simple piece of speech that doesn't resort to figures and a form of speech that is figurative (*figuratus*). I suppose he means that figurative speech demands that we pay particular attention to it, while simple speech hopes to go unnoticed (though that too is a rhetorical ploy). Among the tropes, Quintilian names and describes metaphor, synecdoche, metonymy, and many more. He also distinguishes—at last—figures of speech from figures of thought. Of figures of thought, he instances the rhetorical question, the various ways of anticipating objections (prolepsis), putting words into the mouth of one's adversary, or personifications such as the fatherland (prosopopoeia), and various forms of irony.

Auerbach describes in detail "the strangely new meaning of *figura* in the Christian world," first found in Tertullian. In the *Adversus Marcionem* Tertullian writes of Oshea, son of Nun, whom Moses (according to Numbers 13:16) named Jehoshua (Joshua):

"Et incipit vocari Jesus . . . Hanc prius dicimus figuram futurorum fuisse . . . Petra enim Christus; ideo is vir, qui in huius sacramenti imagines parabatur, etiam nominis dominici inauguratus est figura, Jesus cognominatus" (For the first time he is called Jesus . . . This, then, we first say, was a figure of things to come . . . for Christ is a rock; therefore that man, who was prepared as a type of this sacrament, was even consecrated in figure with the Lord's name and was called Jesus).

Auerbach explains that "the naming of Joshua-Jesus is a phenomenal prophecy or prefiguration of the future Saviour; *figura* is something real and historical which announces something else that is also real and historical." The relation between the two events "is revealed by an accord or similarity."

But this leaves awkwardly open, in Christian thought, the possibly invidious relation between the Old Testament and the New. The relation is metaphorical in the sense that the prophetic or prefiguring events in the Old are deemed to be fulfilled, completed, in the New; but this implies—though Auerbach does not say as much—that the events in the Old Testament suffer a lack that is remedied in the New, as in metaphor, where the tenor—to take up Richards's terms—is completed only by the vehicle and the two parts are somehow held in mind as a double entity. But in some metaphors the richness of detail in the vehicle nearly overwhelms the tenor, and we recall only its penury. Tertullian denied, as Auerbach has it, "that the literal and historical validity of the Old Testament was diminished by the figural interpretation":

> He was definitely hostile to spiritualism and refused to consider the Old Testament as mere allegory; according to him, it had real, literal meaning throughout, and even where there was figural prophecy, the figure had just as much historical reality as what it prophesied. The prophetic figure, he believed, is a concrete historical fact, and it is fulfilled by concrete historical facts. For this Tertullian uses the term *figuram implere,* as in *figuram sanguinis sui salutaris implere,* "to fulfill the figure of his saving blood."[28]

Figure   33

With Tertullian as authority, Auerbach refers to the two events as "figure" and "fulfillment." He emphasizes "how concretely both terms were intended in Tertullian's figural interpretation; in every case the only spiritual factor is the understanding, *intellectus spiritualis*, which recognizes the figure in the fulfillment." In "De baptismo," where the pool of Bethesda appears as a figure of baptism, we find this sentence: "Figura ista medicinae corporalis spiritalem medicinam canebat, ea forma qua simper carnalia in figuram spiritalium antecedent" (This figure of bodily healing told of a spiritual healing, according to the rule by which carnal things come first as a figure of spiritual things). Moses "is no less historical and real because he is an *umbra* or *imago* of Christ, and Christ, the fulfillment, is no abstract idea, but also a historical reality."

There was, however—as there still is—the opposite interpretation: insistently in Origen and Philo, according to whom the events of the Old Testament and indeed some of the New are spiritual rather than historical; they yield to whatever moral or mystical lessons may plausibly be adduced from them. This "spiritualist-ethical-allegorical method," as Auerbach rather coldly calls it, persisted into the Middle Ages side by side with the figural method but not amicably with it; the two are profoundly different. In Origen's method the Old Testament loses "far more of its concrete history than in the figural system." Some theologians call this supersessionism, and take it to justify the claim that Jews could be honored only on condition that they convert to Roman Catholicism, a claim disavowed, belatedly indeed, by Pope Paul VI in his *Nostra Aetate* (October 28, 1965) and *Dignitatis Humanae* (December 7, 1965).[29]

I associate the disagreement between Tertullian and Origen with different ways of reading metaphors. There are Tertullians who treat tenor and vehicle with equal respect, and Origens who regard the vehicle as displacing the tenor and often floating free of it. The vehicle may be respected as surplus knowledge or it may be deemed to be merely an ornamental coloring of the tenor. Some readers hold that the vehicle must count for more than the tenor: if it doesn't redeem the poverty of the tenor, why resort to it? As in Milton's epic similes, the tenor, the entity in hand, maintains its resolute existence, but the vehicle outruns it with apparent freedom and abundance, like a child breaking free of its parents. Some readers denounce the vehicle as a nuisance, for this reason: it obeys no law.

St. Augustine, according to Auerbach, "played a leading part in the compromise between the two doctrines. On the whole he favored a living, figural interpretation, for his thinking was far too concrete and historical to content itself with pure abstract allegory." But I intervene to say that Augustine, at least in *De musica,* regarded music as superior to painting because it was less dependent on the external world. But generally, in Augustine's writings, *figura* continues to mean the visible or audible form of something; it may also mean "the variable aspect over against the imperishable essence." Mostly, it is used to recommend the figural interpretation of the Old Testament. Noah's ark is a prefiguration of the church; Moses is *figura Christi;* Hagar the slave woman is a figure of the Old Testament as Sarah is of the New; Jacob and Esau prefigure the two peoples, Jews and Christians; Hannah's song of praise over the birth of her son Samuel is a figure of the transformation of the old earthly kingdom and priesthood into the new heavenly kingdom and priesthood; she is a *figura ecclesiae.* Joseph Ratzinger refers to these words of the Old Testament, especially "stray" words such as the promise of "Em-

Figure   35

manuel" in Isaiah 7, as words in waiting, opaque until fulfilled in Jesus.[30] But Augustine warned against doubting the historical character of the Old Testament: "When you hear an exposition of the mystery of the Scriptures telling of things that took place, you should believe what is read to have taken place as the reading narrates; lest, undermining the foundation of actuality, you try as it were to build in the air." Christians should hold "to the law of faith, by which the just man lives." The Old Testament is "a promise in figure (*promissio figurata*); the New Testament is a promise understood after the spirit (*spiritualiter intellecta*)." More explicitly in *Contra Faustinum:*

> Temporalium quidem rerum promissiones Testamento Veteri contineri, et ideo Vetus Testamentum appellari nemo nostrum ambigit; et quod aeternae vitae promissio regnumque coelorum ad Novum pertinet Testamentum: sed in illis temporalibus figuras fuisse futurorum quae implerentur in nobis, in quos finis saeculorum obvenit, non suspicio mea, sed apostolicus intellectus est, dicente Paulo, cum de talibus loqueretur: Haec omnia. (For we are all aware that the Old Testament contains promises of temporal things, and that is why it is called the Old Testament; and that the promise of eternal life and the kingdom of heaven belongs to the New Testament: but that in these temporal figures there was the promise of future things, which were to be fulfilled in us, on whom the end of the world is come: this is no fantasy of mine, but the interpretation of the apostles, as Paul says, speaking of these matters.)

But in some respects Paul damaged the figural interpretation, even as he used it in preaching among the gentiles. Auerbach comments: "[Paul's] thinking, which eminently combined practical

politics with creative poetic faith, transformed the Jewish conception of Moses risen again in the Messiah into a system of figural prophecy, in which the risen one both fulfills and annuls the
work of his predecessor."[31]

"Annuls" is the lethal word. Paul's epistles "are intended to
strip the Old Testament of its normative character and show that
it is merely a shadow of things to come." Observance (of the old
law) "has become useless and even harmful since Christ made his
sacrifice; a Christian is justified not by works in observance of the
law, but by faith; in its Jewish and Judaistic legal sense the Old
Testament is the letter that kills, while the new Christians are
servants of the new covenant, of the spirit that gives life." Paul's
version of figural interpretation "changed the Old Testament from
a book of laws and a history of the people of Israel into a series of
figures of Christ and the Redemption." But there is a passage in
Paul's Epistle to the Romans (11:2) that is regularly quoted by
those who regard hostility to Jews as disgusting: "God hath not
cast away his people which he foreknew."[32]

When I was growing up in the church, I didn't notice that the
Old Testament was quietly expunged from the holy books we
were expected to read. We didn't hear a word of it at Mass. We
were instructed only in the New Testament, with emphasis on
the parables. At school we had a book called *Apologetics and Catholic Doctrine*. Outside school, a priest gave me a gift of St. Thomas
à Kempis's *Imitation of Christ*. (My father was angry that I accepted
it. I should keep my distance from priests, except for their place in
the church, Mass, and the sacraments). But the Old Testament
might as well—or better—not have existed. One of the consequences of the second Vatican Council is that we now hear a passage of the Old Testament as the first reading at Mass.

Figure   37

Auerbach shows, in his interpretation of the church fathers, that while the accredited meaning of *figura* was "form" and referred to qualities neutral if not noble, it could also slide into an imputation of "mere form," deception, as of a wolf hiding in a sheep's clothing. In extravagances of metaphor, figures that draw attention to themselves are easily resented as vainglorious, especially if the humble practice of calling a spade a spade is to be respected. In this mode, *figura* was often contrasted with *truth* (*veritas*) rather than seen as foretelling a higher truth. Other words were sometimes used instead of *figura;* the commonest synonyms were *ambages, effigies, exemplum, imago, similitudo, species,* and *umbra. Exemplum* would be used, I assume, when a moral lesson was to be drawn, as in 1 Cor. 10:11: "Now all these things happened unto them for ensamples: and they are written for our admonition, upon whom the ends of the world are come." But Auerbach makes it clear that none of these words "combined the elements of the concept so fully as *figura:* the creative, formative principle, change amid the enduring essence, the shades of meaning between copy and archetype."

Figural interpretation, as Auerbach describes it, "establishes a connection between two events or persons, the first of which signifies not only itself but also the second, while the second encompasses or fulfills the first." The trouble is that the "second" by definition has the last word: to encompass is to win. Or the penultimate word, if not the last one, for as Auerbach notes:

> Every future model, though incomplete as history, is already fulfilled in God and has existed from all eternity in His providence. The figures in which He cloaked it, and the Incarnation in which He revealed its meaning, are therefore prophecies of

something that has always been, but which will remain veiled to men and women until the day when they behold the Saviour *revelata facie,* with the senses as well as in spirit.[33]

The sacrament of the Eucharist, "the Last Supper, the *pascha nostrum,* which is the *figura Christi*" makes it clear that "this sacrament, which is figure as well as symbol, and which has long existed historically—namely, since it was first established in the old covenant—gives us the purest picture of the concretely present, the veiled and tentative, the eternal and supratemporal elements contained in the figures."

The culmination of Auerbach's essay is the revision of his book on Dante (1929). When he wrote it, he says, he did not have a sufficient historical grounding for his interpretation of *The Divine Comedy:*

> I believe that I have now [1944] found this historical grounding; it is precisely the figural interpretation of reality which, though in constant conflict with purely spiritualist and Neoplatonic tendencies, was the dominant view in the European Middle Ages: the idea that earthly life is thoroughly real, with the reality of the flesh into which the Logos entered, but that with all its reality it is only *umbra* and *figura* of the authentic, future, ultimate truth, the real reality that will unveil and preserve the *figura.*[34]

Of Dante's descriptions of Beatrice, Auerbach says—"Beatrice is incarnation, she is *figura* or *idolo Christi* (her eyes reflect her two-fold nature, *Purgatorio* 31,126) and thus she is not exhausted by such explanations; her relation to Dante cannot fully be explained by dogmatic considerations." The figural interpretation of reality, like

Figure   39

the relation of the Old Testament to the New, for Christians, is a metaphorical relation, incomparably for many centuries the fundamental act of mind by which Christians made sense of their lives on earth and their hope for a future life in the presence of God. No other metaphorical relation has such richness of promise. Even now, when the senses of *figura* have to be restored, reconstituted, the word retains at least some of its old latitude of ramification. Gadamer was following in Auerbach's footsteps when be said, in *Truth and Method,* that "it is the prejudice of a theory of logic that is alien to language if the metaphorical use of a word is regarded as not its real sense."[35]

But the notion of fulfillment, as in the New Testament fulfilling the Old, has its problems, especially if it implies that the relation between the two testaments is a quiet, complete transition. Newman has complicated this motif by pointing out that "though Our Lord claims to be the Messiah, He shows so little of conscious dependence on the old Scriptures, or of anxiety to fulfill them; as if it became Him, who was the Lord of the Prophets, to take His own course, and to leave their utterances to adjust themselves to Him as they could, and not to be careful to accommodate Himself to them":

> He Himself goes straight forward on His way, of course claiming to be the Messiah of the Prophets, still not so much recurring to past prophecies, as uttering new ones, with an antithesis not unlike that which is so impressive in the Sermon on the Mount, when He first says, "It has been said by them of old time," and then adds, "But I say unto you." In those two names, Son of God and Son of Man, declaratory of the two natures of Emmanuel, He separates Himself from the

Jewish Dispensation, in which He was born, and inaugurates
the New Covenant.[36]

This does not invalidate the motif of fulfillment, but it speaks
boldly to the interruptive force of Christ and the apostles and what
Newman calls "the independent autocratic view which [Christ]
takes of His own religion, into which the old Judaism was melting."[37] It also complicates any sense we may have received of equi-
poise between figure and fulfillment, prophecy and event.

Of the hymns I sang in Warrenpoint, the "Adoro te devote" is the
one I most shake my head over. I had not the least idea of what I
was singing. Surely someone, Mr. Crawford, Father McMullan,
Canon McAllister—no, not the dreaded Canon, or the sad priest
who gave me the *Imitation of Christ*—might have explained to me
what the first two stanzas of Aquinas's Latin are about:

> Adore te devote, latens deitas
> Quae sub his figuris vere latitas
> Tibi se cor meum totum subiicit
> Quia te contemplans totum deficit.
>
> Visus, tactus, gustus in te fallitur
> Sed audito solo tuto creditur:
> Credo quidquid dixit Dei filius:
> Nil hoc verbo veritatis verius.

I've already given Peter Walsh's translation of the first stanza; here
is his second:

> The sight, the touch, the taste are all in you deceived;
> but to my ears alone I safely lend belief.

Figure   41

All that the son of God has said, I do believe;

nothing is truer than the word of truth himself. (p. 367).

In 1648, or earlier, Richard Crashaw understood Aquinas well enough to elaborate on this hymn "in adoration of the Blessed Sacrament." While he added lines in the spirit of the original but not found in Aquinas's text, he ignored—or took for granted, as beneath his notice—the quandary of "sub his figuris vere latitas." Hopkins was more attentive to "God in these bare shapes, poor shadows, darkling now." Crashaw struck the senses down, except for the sense of hearing:

Down down, proud sense! Discourses dy.

Keep close, my soul's inquiring ey!

Nor touch nor tast must look for more

But each sitt still in his own Dore.

Your ports are all superfluous here,

Save That which lets in faith, the eare.

Faith is my skill. Faith can believe

As fast as love new lawes can give.

Faith is my force. Faith strength affords

To keep pace with those powrfull words.

And words more sure, more sweet, then they

ʼLove could not think, truth could not say.[38]

Shouting "Faith" four times is not quite as convincing as Aquinas's "Credo quidquid dixit Dei filius," with its irrefutable rhyme on "verius" and its relegation of "visus, tactus, gustus" as inadequate instruments for the reception of faith. The contrast between this Thomas, who believed on the strength of hearing the Word, and the doubting one who demanded to see and touch before believing is also clearer in Aquinas than in Crashaw. Not that I understand why we are given at least five senses but told that four of them are no good for the reception of faith: when Jesus appeared to the eleven apostles after the crucifixion, he said, "Peace be unto you," but he also showed them his hands and his side. And aren't we promised, in 1 Cor. 13:12, that in heaven we shall see God "face to face"? This is the most daring of metaphors, justified only by Paul's prophetic zeal.

One passage in particular, at the end of "Adoro te devote," makes me feel particularly dismayed that I did not know what I was singing:

> Pie pelicane, Jesu domine
> Me immundum munda tuo sanguine
> Cuius una stilla salvum facere
> Totum mundum quit ab omne scelere
> Jesum quem velatum nunc aspicio
> Oro: fiat illud quod tam cupio,
> Ut te revelata cernens facie
> Visu sim beatus tuae gloriae.

As if to pray, in Crashaw's version:

> O soft self-wounding Pelican!
> Whose brest weepes Balm for wounded man.
> Ah this way bend thy benign floud
> To'a bleeding Heart that gaspes for blood.
> That blood, whose least drops soveraign be
> To wash my worlds of sin from me.
> Come love! Come LORD! And that long day
> For which I languish, come away.

Figure   43

When this dry soul those eyes shall see,
And drink the unseal'd sourse of thee.
When Glory's sun faith's shades shall chase,
And for thy veil give me thy FACE.[39]

Or in Hopkins's more alliterative version:

Like what tender tales tell of the Pelican;
Bathe me, Jesu Lord, in what thy bosom ran—
Blood that but one drop of has the worth to win
All the world forgiveness of its world of sin.

Jesu whom I look at veilèd here below,
I beseech thee send me what I thirst for so,
Some day to gaze on thee face to face in light
And be blest for ever with thy glory's sight.[40]

It is typical of Hopkins to change Aquinas's vision and Crashaw's languishing into "thirst."

Surely someone might have explained to me what Aquinas's pelican metaphor is doing, and the acoustic value—though not just that—of passing from "panis" to "vivus" to "vitam," and the wordplay of "praestans" and "praesta," the rhymes of "domini" and "homini," of "vivere" and "sapere," the alliterative quibble of "me immundum munda," the figurative force of "velatum" set off against "revelata cernens facie." It would have been gratifying to learn that the "Pie pelicane" is there because the bird is represented in medieval art and heraldry, when food fails, as tearing her breast in order to feed her young with her blood: hence the pelican was taken as a symbol of Christ. I never knew that. In Ireland I was inclined to think that "pius" means "holy" as well as dutiful, since many Catholics were said to be pious, and many popes were named Pius. But even when I lived in Dublin as a student, I did not advert to the fact that the headquarters of the blood transfusion service was Pelican House. It is a late pleasure to forage among the evidences. I quote a few of them.

Psalm 102:6 has a pelican from a strange myth: "I am like a pelican of the wilderness: I am like an owl of the desert." That is the King James version, but I note that Robert Alter translates it as "I resemble the wilderness jackdaw, I become like the owl of the ruins," on the grounds that "as with many biblical terms for fauna, the exact identity of this sad nocturnal bird is uncertain."[41] In *Paradiso* there is the exquisite moment when Beatrice sees the brightened splendor—*lo schiarato splendore*—of John, the disciple whom Jesus loved:

> "Questi è colui che giacque sopra 'l petto
>> del nostro pellicano, e questi fue
>> di su la croce al grande officio eletto."

(This is he who lay upon the breast of our Pelican, and this is he who was chosen from upon the Cross for the great office [of caring for Mary the mother of Jesus]; Dante, *Paradiso* 25, 112–114, translation by Charles S. Singleton). Laertes, being challenged by Claudius to distinguish friends from enemies, talks nonsense near to blasphemy:

> To his [Polonius's] good friends thus wide I'll ope my arms;
> And like the kind life-rend'ring pelican,
> Repast them with my blood. (Shakespeare, *Hamlet*,
>> IV.v.145–147)

In Shakespeare's *Richard II* John of Gaunt, rebuking the king and virtually accusing him of the murder of the Duke of Gloucester, mixes his metaphors without losing a point:

Figure   45

O, spare me not, my brother Edward's son,

For that I was his father Edward's son;

That blood already, like the pelican,

Hast thou tapp'd out and drunkenly caroused:

My brother Gloucester, plain well-meaning soul. (II.i.124–128)

Yeats writes, in "A General Introduction for My Work":

I commit my emotion to shepherds, herdsmen, camel-drivers, learned men, Milton's or Shelley's Platonist, that tower [Samuel] Palmer drew. Talk to me of originality and I will turn on you with rage. I am a crowd, I am a lonely man, I am nothing. Ancient salt is best packing. The heroes of Shakespeare convey to us through their looks, or through the metaphorical patterns of their speech, the sudden enlargement of their vision, their ecstasy at the approach of death: "She should have died hereafter," "Of many thousand kisses, the poor last," "Absent thee from felicity awhile." They have become God or Mother Goddess, the pelican, "My baby at my breast," but all must be cold; no actress has ever sobbed when she played Cleopatra.[42]

Lear, denouncing Goneril and Regan as ingrates, says: "Judicious punishment! 'twas this flesh begot / Those pelican daughters" (Shakespeare, *King Lear,* III.iv.77). This refers to another part of the story of pelicans: that when the children start to grow up, they hit the parents in the face with their wings. Lear doesn't persist in the story. The parents, striking back, kill their children. Three days later, the mother pierces her breast, opens her side, and lays herself across her young, pouring out her blood over their dead bodies, thus bringing them to life again. In a bestiary of the twelfth century we read:

> In the same way, Our Lord Jesus Christ . . . begets us and calls
> us into being out of nothing. We, on the contrary, strike him
> in the face. As the prophet Isaiah says: "I have borne children
> and exalted them and truly they have scorned me." We have
> struck him in the face by devoting ourselves to the creation
> rather than the creator. . . . That was why he ascended into
> the height of the cross, and, his side having been pierced,
> there came from it blood and water for our salvation and eter-
> nal life.[43]

But in Aquinas's hymn there are no children, only "Pie pellicane," the mother bird, and its sacrificial mercy.

Aquinas says in *De Veritate:*

> In matters dealing with God there are two different ways of
> speaking: (1) In proper language. This is found when we attri-
> bute to God what pertains to Him in His own nature, although
> it always pertains to Him in a way that goes beyond what we
> conceive in our minds or express in speech. For this reason
> none of our language about God can be proper in the full sense:
> (2) to speak in figurative, transferred, or symbolic language.
> Because God, as He is in himself, exceeds the grasp of our
> mind, we must speak of Him by means of the things that are
> found in our world. So we apply to God the names of sensible
> things, calling Him a light or a lion or something of the sort.[44]

Aquinas's first consideration opens the door again, already opened
by the pseudo-Dionysus, to "negative theology" in which the
theologian expresses his relation to God by saying, helplessly,
what he knows he is not. Aquinas's second consideration makes

Figure   47

metaphor hopeless, where God is the object of speech but sustainably hopeless: it makes the best of an impossible situation. Donne, Andrewes, and other divines deal with this ruefully but not to the extent of lapsing into silence. The situation is possible only because Christ was at once God and man.

In rhetoric Aquinas's "Adoro te" would be called an apostrophe, as when a speaker turns aside to address a present or absent entity or makes an address in more direct terms than usual. Milton's hymn to light ("Hail Holy Light") at the beginning of the third Book of *Paradise Lost* is such an apostrophe. It might just as well be called a prayer. Aquinas gives the vehicle first; the tenor follows in the name of Jesus, both in the vocative case. The juxtaposition makes a metaphor because there is a transfer of force from Jesus to pelican, though in the evoked symbolism the feeling can go both ways. The four lines rhyme as couplets, the rhyming words each with three syllables. The main character of the verse is the alliteration of "me immundum munda," followed by the play of "salvum," "totum," and "mundum." There is a stronger play of sense between "immundum" (unclean) and the imperative verb "munda" (cleanse). Staying with "Pie pellicane": I translate "Pie" as dutiful, because the relation between the bird and its young is protective, issuing from an innate sense of duty. Pelicans don't protect other birds, only their own young. There is no "is," no predicate between vehicle and tenor. Nor is the relation between them one of likeness. Christ is not like a pelican. The relation is one of mythic and cultural congruity. The pelican's protectiveness to its young, at grievous cost to itself, is one instance, in a nature often red in tooth and claw, of a saving "current of energy," as Frye puts it, between the human and the natural worlds. Is it Christ's duty, then, to save human beings, at whatever personal cost? Yes, it is a duty he has accepted, as sacrifice, from his father. Are Christ and the pelican identified by the metaphor? No, but they are made to inhabit the same space, the "here" and "now." It is up to each reader to determine what that *habitus* comes to.

To sum up, if only provisionally: God chose to hide himself, "Que Dieu s'est voulu cacher," as Pascal wrote, translating Isaiah 45.15 as "Véritablement tu es un Dieu caché."[45] Presumably He chose to hide himself so that one day He would reveal himself, show His face to the elect. This readily lends itself to the Christian emphasis on the future and the end of time. Meanwhile God conceals himself *sub his figuris,* these figures being words in the two founding books—the Bible and nature. The Bible is a book of acts and agencies. Nature is a constellation of readable signs: a sign, as C. S. Peirce said, is "something by knowing which we know something more."[46] Things in the world become signs when we reach out to them as such. Or rather, they become utterances. When we lean and hearken to them, they become things said that say other things in their turn: audible figures. In *The Rule of Metaphor* Ricoeur says that language "raises the experience of the world to its articulation in discourse, that which founds communication and brings about the advent of man as speaking subject."[47] Figures of speech and figures of thought are acts of the mind by which we pay attention to parts of the world; we call the capacity of those acts imagination when they are not limited to reference or allusion to what is already there. In the *Critique of Judgment* Kant says that when reason, the understanding, and concepts fail, imagination—the life-giving principle of mind—forces the mind to think beyond itself.[48] Gaston Bachelard maintained that "we always think of the imagination as the faculty that *forms* images:

Figure   49

on the contrary, it *deforms* what we perceive."[49] In literature, the only limits are those of language. If something is not possible in language, it is not possible at all; though by "language" here I mean not just common usage or even formal, syntactical speech and writing but extravagances such as *Finnegans Wake,* the *Alice* books, and the writings of Edward Lear. If something is possible in language, it is possible at least as a mental entity, a picture, and therefore a figure. Semblances can be adumbrated in language, even if they do not otherwise exist. Heidegger's "flute-playing centaur" is not to be found in the world, but a semblance of it exists because he imagined it and brought it forward. Figures in the world are therefore instruments but not ignoble in that capacity. In the *Phaedrus,* Socrates speaks of the soul in a figure, a composite figure of a pair of winged horses driven by a charioteer. In "The Noble Rider and the Sound of Words" Wallace Stevens quotes Socrates and estimates the current status of the figure, concluding that it has lost its vitality because in it "the imagination adheres to what is unreal."[50] If Stevens is right about Socrates's composite figure, it follows that figures may lose their value not because they wilt of themselves but because our relation to them declines. This may be a version of one of Auerbach's themes, whether the figures in the Old Testament are annulled or even diminished by having their fulfillment in the New. The Ten Commandments are not—or not necessarily—diminished by comparison with the Beatitudes, unless we take fulfillment to entail supersession. Does a metaphor demean the tenor by declaring what it lacks? Is it shamed by that consideration?

A figurative sense of life deviates from that sense of it which is sustained by common usages of language. Not that these usages are despicable: we could not live without them; they account for every form of conviviality. But it is also natural, or at least cultural, to imagine deviating from them, living as if at a distance from their seductions.

What I learned from Auerbach's essay was something he did not quite say: that the most consequential figure in the history of rhetoric is the metaphor by which the Old Testament is fulfilled—or abrupted, challenged—in the New. The standard account of a metaphor is that it entails speaking of something as if it were something else. The newly created fish, in Milton's *Paradise Lost,* disport themselves as if they were girls learning to flirt:

> Part single or with mate
> Graze the seaweed their pasture, and through groves
> Of coral stray, or sporting with quick glance
> Show to the sun their waved coats dropped with gold,
> Or in their pearly shells at ease, attend
> Moist nutriment. (VII. 403–8)

The standard reason for a metaphor is to deny that the thing mentioned is entirely or merely what it is commonly deemed to be: it may have qualities you've never thought of. You have never thought of fish as showing themselves—showing off—to the sun, "sporting with quick glance," displaying their waved coats— waved, undulant—dropped with gold, dotted with gold spots. You are not obliged to think of them in this guise; you may reject the lines as trivial. But you would be reading the poem against the grain of it if you refused, even for a second, to think of the fish as flirts. You might decide, on second thoughts, to dismiss the metaphor as Milton's showing off, and to continue reading the poem free of any such interpretive obligation. But this is freedom you can exercise in reading anything.

Figure   51

The fathers of the church were adept in turning the events of the Old Testament to theological purpose. They respected those events while giving them a metaphorical destiny. Taking them as the first part of a metaphor—the tenor—they completed the metaphor by transforming it—this is the vehicle—into the supposedly corresponding episode in Christendom. This had the immediate effect of emphasizing the interruptive character of Christianity while respecting the tradition that made the interruption—and the metaphor—possible. Paul wrote to the Romans that "whatsoever things were written aforetime were written for our learning, that we through patience and comfort of the scriptures might have hope" (Romans 15:4).

Tertullian's account of the relation between the Old Testament and the New is the most comprehensive metaphor in the history of rhetoric. It follows that the essential character of metaphor is prophetic. Metaphors offer to change the world by changing one's sense of it. The best metaphors are revolutionary, not merely descriptive—although descriptions too may be revelations.

After Aristotle

Original pieces of thinking have, I suppose, nearly
always been started on metaphor, and so far from
being peculiarly "emotive" and indulgent of folly, a
metaphor is often a loophole for common sense; when
a man is dutifully deceiving himself he will often
admit the truth in his metaphor.

—William Empson

i find in Gustav Stern's *Meaning and Change of Meaning
with Special Reference to the English Language* (1931) definitions of
simile and metaphor that are more elaborate than Richards's. "A
simile consists in the formal and avowed comparison of one thing
to another." A metaphor is "a figure of speech in which (1) the
enhancement is the result of a fusion between two disparate notions, *i.e.,* there is no essential identity between the two referents
involved; and (2) the relation between the two referents is not
expressed."[1] "Fusion" is not helpful, it sets up a new problem by
being itself a metaphor. The two disparate notions or referents
will now be called, after Richards, tenor and vehicle. Enhancement is a good word to indicate why the writer or speaker re-
sorted to a metaphor at all; she wouldn't have done so if she had
been content to say, "the cat is on the mat." "No essential identity":
true, no identity, essential or not. The relation between tenor and

vehicle "is not expressed": is not explicit, it remains to be divined by readers or listeners:

> The metaphor expresses shades of thought and feeling which could not otherwise be formulated in speech, or not so concisely and precisely formulated. The value of a metaphor lies in the adding of new attributes to a referent, its placing in a net of new complex relations, through which it is brought into a new light, receives peculiar emotional values and is comprehended more vividly and completely than before.[2]

The only part of that passage I'm not happy with is "adding." The vehicle is not added to the tenor. Metaphor is the mutual relation of tenor and vehicle, a relation achieved by holding the two simultaneously in one's mind. How that is done is a puzzle.

Sometimes the difference between a simile and a metaphor is not clear. The narrator of Nabokov's *Despair* goes for a walk: "It was a fast, fresh, blue-dappled day; the wind, a distant relation of the one here, winged its course along the narrow streets; a cloud every now and then palmed the sun, which reappeared like a conjurer's coin."[3] "Like a conjurer's coin" seems to be a simile, but "palmed" takes first possession of the experience and appropriates the likeness into a state close to identity: a metaphor, I would say. But the whole sentence tells us more about the narrator's way of looking at things than it does about cloud and sun. Richards's tenor and vehicle don't apply. What we are made especially aware of is the narrator's way of turning natural events into cultural ones. Later in the novel, the narrator and his double are having a meal and a drink in a rotten eating house that included "the distant bar at which a man drank, legs twisted into a black scroll, and smoke encircling him"[4]—a metaphor because the relation between the man's legs and a black scroll is not mere likeness; the scroll has taken over the scene. The narrator sees the man's legs as a black scroll when no one else in the world would see them as that. The relation belongs to the narrator and to him alone. It is a subjective metaphor inasmuch as it is an attribute of the narrator's mind and of no one else's.

Suppose that an early-middle-aged man named J. Alfred Prufrock brought himself to the point, reluctantly indeed, of paying a visit to a friend. He has something difficult to say to her, so he brings a companion along to spread the risk. He anticipates that the lady will not appreciate what he has to say and that she will thwart his efforts by interrupting him: "That is not what I meant at all, that is not it, at all." Even before the friends arrive at the lady's residence, Prufrock knows that he will not be able to explain his case. "It is impossible to say just what I mean," he protests to himself or to his companion. But he tries, perhaps failing again or failing better, as Beckett said, "But as if a magic lantern threw the nerves in patterns on a screen." That doesn't sound promising. "As if" is nearly hopeless, where clarity is required, but at least it is a start, the start of a metaphor, an attempt to give "what I mean" a chance to clarify itself or to escape its predicament by recourse to a different range of words. It softens the metaphor by reducing the claim it exerts. Empson thought that people invent metaphors "when the conscious mind has its eye on a few important elements in the situation and the classifying subconscious is called on for a suggestive word."[5] My Prufrock may have thought of nerves because he felt his own to be in disarray, and then he may have adverted to the magic lantern as a device for imposing some degree of order on them, such a pattern being the best he could hope for, however mechanical. To devise a metaphor, in that case, may have entailed a desperate resolve to deal with his situation by at least nominally getting out of it. An act of will would be entailed, as it always is in metaphor. Now suppose further that Prufrock stumbled on the image of a magic lantern and hoped it might serve his purpose. No one had thought of it before; it is his invention for this local purpose, a discovery among the words of the English language, good or bad. Suppose further still that his metaphor, however implausibly, happens to come into the public domain. Someone hears of it, it catches on, or it doesn't. If it doesn't, it's never heard of again; if it does, other people start using it; it becomes fashionable, especially among those who like to talk about their nerves. It becomes a part of common speech, like the heart of the matter, in the fullness of time, the leg of the table, the heel of the hunt, comfort zone, brass tacks, the leaf of the book, picture of health, a wild-goose chase, presence of mind, creature of habit, towering oaks, wolf in sheep's clothing, Freudian slip, no-win situation, toxic assets, push comes to shove, or any of the thousands of such phrases that were once discoveries— most of them metaphors—phrases once in high repute. After a while of years or decades, people who think themselves socially advanced begin to make fun of the magic lantern metaphor. They start thinking it stupid or vulgar. They use it only with their friends as an irony. They regard it as a dead metaphor, and avoid it. But commoners still use it, to show off. It has now receded into usage. After more decades, it is still in easy use. Everybody has forgotten that it is a metaphor. They think it is just part of the vernacular, as indeed it is. According to Nietzsche, it has even become accepted as an ordinary statement of truth. What is truth? he asks:

> A movable host of metaphors, metonymies, and anthropo-
> morphisms: in short: a sum of human relations which have
> been poetically and rhetorically intensified, transferred, and
> embellished, and which, after long usage, seem to a people to
> be fixed, canonical, and binding. Truths are illusions which
> we have forgotten are illusions; they are metaphors that have
> become worn out and have been drained of sensuous force.[6]

Common usage depends on phrases that were once metaphors
but whose glowing origin has been forgotten. When I complain
to someone that he sent me on a wild-goose chase, I know what
I'm saying, and so does he, but I've no idea what the original
point of a wild-goose chase was or how it became a metaphor. If
I say that "inflation will wreak havoc on my pension," I know
what I mean but I've long forgotten how wreaking havoc comes
into my speech. So I consult the OED and learn that "cry havoc"
refers to the order an officer gives his troops to seize spoil and to
plunder the conquered village or town. Hence in Shakespeare's
Julius Caesar Antony's threat:

> And Caesar's spirit, ranging for revenge,
> With Ate by his side come hot from hell,
> Shall in these confines with a monarch's voice
> Cry "Havoc," and let slip the dogs of war. (III.1.270–273)

But I don't know when "havoc" became a free-for-all. I know
what inflation will do to my pension. If I say "It never dawned on
me that he could be such a boor," I have forgotten how "dawned"
came to be figurative. The first use of it known to the OED in
that sense—"to begin to become evident to the mind"—comes
from *Uncle Tom's Cabin:* "The idea that they had either feelings or

rights had never dawned upon her." This sounds improbable; surely it became a metaphor before 1852. Maybe it had begun to subside into middle-class speech before Mrs. Stowe used it.

This doesn't mean that "wreak havoc" or "play havoc" are dead metaphors. There are no dead metaphors, only sleeping ones: any of them, looking like death, can be brought to life by paying attention to it. If you hover over a word or a phrase instead of drifting along its surface, you bring the sleeping thing back to life, usually by deforming it or emphasizing it, as in a pun. One's consciousness is the crucial intervention in restoring an apparently dead metaphor to life. Karl Kraus, thinking of Hitler's persecution of the Jews, wrote that "to pour salt in open wounds" had ceased to be a metaphor, because the metaphor had been "reabsorbed by its reality."[7]

In a quieted tone, suppose I were to say to someone what an opulent leg your table has; Jack's become quite a Cubist picture of health; I'm an epicure of habit; he's a sporting wolf in a sheep's suit; I'll prove the emphatic presence of my mind in a New York minute; I'll chase that wild goose if you want me to; all things generously considered; those assets taste a bit toxic to me, the metaphors wouldn't be quite as dead as they had seemed. "Sleight of hand" is all that remains of the sleight that for centuries was featured in relation to many other organs—sleight of heart, for instance—but in the poem "Come In," Frost thought of a thrush in dark woods trying "by sleight of wing" to better its perch for the night. In "Infanta Marina," Stevens imagined a creature of the evening, the rumpling of whose plumes "Came to be sleights of sails / Over the sea."

Coleridge recommended tracing a word to its origin as a device for activating it; any form of attention to it is enough. He also made a great Unitarian fuss about mistaking metaphor for reality:

The next Corruption which took place among Christians is the doctrine of Redemption. While the Jewish Ceremonies were still existing, or fresh in the memory of men, the scriptural allusions to them and figures of Speech built upon them escaped misinterpretation. But when their City and Sanctuary were destroyed, and the study of the Jewish Antiquities had become less and less fashionable, the Similes of the New Testament were made to signify the thing assimilated, and Metaphors consolidated into realities.[8]

And in another place, thinking of Spenser's "Errour," he wrote this note:

The understanding of Metaphor for Reality (Loaves and Fishes=Apostles, Fisherman, Christ's Doctrine /&c &c) one of the Foundations of the many-headed River of Credulity which overflowing covers the world with miscreations & reptile monsters, & then gives its huge supply thro' its many mouths into the Sea of Blood.[9]

But the distinction between metaphor and reality is more easily made at the beginning of a metaphor's history. Later, the figure is well on the way to becoming a word or a phrase in the vernacular, at which point it constitutes reality by being the standard expression of it. Jesus took care to indicate that a parable was about to emerge by saying, in each case, "The Kingdom of Heaven is likened to a . . ." Montaigne made fun of rhetoricians and grammarians by saying that when you hear them talk about metonymies, metaphors, allegories, and the like, you think they are referring to some exotic forms of speech, but these words are just like the babble of one's chambermaid. True, but my chambermaid

doesn't know the idiolect she's so volubly babbling; it's her native
tongue. I'm trying to cope with strange idiolects.

The understanding of metaphor has been inordinately governed
by a few sentences that Aristotle jotted down, sometime between
the years 360 and 355 if Gerald F. Else is right, probably as lecture
notes for his *Poetics,* and a more concentrated few for his handbook of civic communication, the *Rhetoric,* which he may have
written around the same time as the *Poetics.*[10] Aristotle (384–322)
was a *rhetor* of prosaic disposition, the inventor of logic, a biologist
by avocation, combative to a fault. He was one of Plato's pupils,
as Stephen Dedalus reminded his companions in the National
Library, inciting John Eglinton to call him "a model schoolboy
with his diploma under his arm." He was a scientist at heart. The
author of the *Poetics* was not a poet, a dramatist, or even by modern description a literary or a theatre critic. His main concern in
the *Poetics* was to defend poetry against the indictment that Plato
brought upon poets in Book 10 of the *Republic*—that they are mere
imitators of reality, and besides, they merely cater to our emotions.
Aristotle undertook to submit Homer—his chief of poets—and
Sophocles's *Oedipus Rex* and other tragedies to a commentary at
once clear and sober. His *Rhetoric* was intended as a guide for those
who would engage in public debate. If a wilder philosopher such
as Heraclitus or Empedocles had written treatises on poetry and
rhetoric—assuming they survived as Aristotle's did—much of West-
ern thought on these subjects would have taken on a flamboyant
rather than a reticent tone—or if Longinus's thoughts on "the
Sublime" had attained central rather than marginal status among
aestheticians. In any event, the *Poetics* was translated into Arabic
by Abu bis Matta, in the early tenth century, from a lost Syriac

translation of a lost Greek original. It became an object of commentary and interpretation—in corrupt texts, admittedly—notably by Avicenna about 1020 and Averroes about 1174.[11] It is unlikely that Aquinas, who wrote commentaries on Aristotle's *Posterior Analytics* and several of his other treatises, took any interest in the *Poetics*. It did not come into the culture of the West until the fifteenth century in Italy and later in France, England, and other countries. Since then, it has retained its status as the text to be argued about or at least to begin with. This may be explained by the fact that Aristotle's philosophy is predicated on a relation between knowledge and action.

On a personal note, when I enrolled to read for a BA degree at University College, Dublin, I found that four books were prescribed as introductions to honors English: Aristotle's *Poetics,* Coleridge's *Biographia Literaria,* Newman's *The Idea of a University,* and Arnold's *On Translating Homer.* Aristotle was respectable because Aquinas annotated him and Aquinas was the church's accredited philosopher. The *Biographia Literaria* was as much philosophy as we were thought to need, enhanced as it was by Coleridge's readings of Shakespeare and Wordsworth—Wordsworth the last major poet we would be obliged to read, more recent literature being, as C. S. Lewis was supposed to have said, "just books." University College was a constituent college of the National University of Ireland, a civic institution that retained a dim recollection of the Catholic university that Newman tried to establish in Dublin in 1851. Most of the students were Roman Catholic in the only sense that mattered in Ireland at the time: they weren't Protestants. *The Idea of a University* advocated the pursuit of knowledge for its own sake and examined other questions that might be included in a draft report on university education, but it was

mainly occupied in presenting the idea of a gentleman and suggesting that a university should take pains to produce such a person. Newman assumed that a university would imitate the form
of an Oxford college. He had nothing to say about a modern, urban
university like University College, Dublin, which undertook to
instruct several thousand students in the practices of medicine,
commerce, architecture, engineering, and liberal studies. *The Idea of
a University* was prescribed, I feel sure, because Jeremiah J. Hogan,
our professor of English, wanted to retain the notion that the college was still, in spirit, Newman's Catholic University. I found the
book far more remote than the *Poetics*. I did not aspire to become,
in Newman's sense or any other, a gentleman. As for *On Translating
Homer,* it was in the syllabus mainly to indicate why Greece mattered and what literary criticism should sound like. Without *On
Translating Homer,* we would probably never have learned how the
word *rapid* could indicate a value in literary criticism.

I quote now the most salient of Aristotle's lecture notes on metaphor, culled from the *Poetics* and the *Rhetoric*. It is convenient to
give them in three parts, since they are separated in the original:

> Metaphor is the application of an alien name by transference
> either from genus to species, or from species to genus, or from
> species to species, or by analogy, that is, proportion. Thus from
> genus to species, as: "There lies my ship," for lying at anchor is
> a species of lying: From species to genus, as: "verily ten thou-
> sand noble deeds hath Odysseus wrought," for "ten thousand"
> is a species of large number, and is here used for a large number
> generally. From species to species, as: "With blade of bronze
> drew away the life," and "Cleft the water with the vessel of
> unyielding bronze." . . . Analogy or proportion is when the

second term is to the first as the fourth to the third. We may then use the fourth for the second, or the second for the fourth. Sometimes too we qualify the metaphor by adding the term to which the proper word is relative. Thus the cup is to Dionysus as the shield to Ares. The cup may therefore be called "the shield of Dionysus," and the shield "the cup of Ares." Or again, as old age is to life, so is evening to day. Evening may therefore be called "the old-age of the day," and old-age "the evening of life," or, in the phrase of Empedocles, "life's setting sun." For some of the terms of the proportion there is at times no word in existence; still the metaphor may be used. For instance, to scatter seed is calling sowing: but the action of the sun in scattering its rays is nameless. Still, this process bears to the sun the same relation as sowing to the seed. Hence the expression of the poet: "sowing the god-created light."

Two or three paragraphs later, Aristotle writes:

> By deviating in exceptional cases from the normal idiom, the language will gain distinction; while, at the same time, the partial conformity with usage will give perspicuity. It is a great matter to observe propriety in these several modes of expression, as also in compound words, strange (or rare) words, and so forth. But the greatest thing by far is to have a command of metaphor. This alone cannot be imparted by another; it is the mark of genius, for to make good metaphors implies an eye for resemblances.[12]

By "an eye for resemblances" Aristotle probably meant more than the common ability to see that something was like something else. He probably meant a flair for seeing likeness between relations involving them. As Hannah Arendt explains:

We know that *noeomai* was first used in the sense of perceiving by the eyes, then transferred to perceptions of the mind in the sense of "apprehend"; finally it became a word for the highest form of thinking. Nobody, we can assume, thought that the eye, the organ of vision, and the *nous,* the organ of thinking, were the same; but the word itself indicated that the relation between the eye and the seen object was similar to the relation between the mind and its thought-object—namely, yielded the same kind of evidence.[13]

Some comments in the *Rhetoric* are repeated from the *Poetics.* Only one of the new passages seems to me inspiring:

It is necessary to say what we mean by bringing-before-the-eyes and what makes this occur. I call those things "before the eyes" that signify things engaged in an activity. For example, to say that a good man is "foursquare" is a metaphor, for both are complete; but it does not signify activity [*energeia*]. But the phrase "having his prime of life in full bloom" is *energeia.* . . . And Homer often uses it, making the lifeless live through the metaphor: in all his work, he gains his fame by creating activity, for example in the following: "Then to the plain rolled the ruthless stone."[14]

Christine Brooke-Rose has remarked that "Aristotle is not very perceptive in making metaphor by analogy into a separate category since analogy applies to all metaphor."[15] I'll extract from these passages the ones that seem to me most telling, and comment on them.

Metaphor is the transfer of a word from its proper or ordinary position in a sentence or a phrase to a position alien to that or distant from it. Aristotle speaks of it mostly as if the word transferred were a noun, but it need not be. In modern poetry, it's often a verb, as in Valéry's "La mer fidèle y dort sur mes tombeaux!" in "Le Cimetière marin." You could derive from Aristotle two theories: that metaphor substitutes one word for another; or that it is entirely a figure of resemblance. As Coleridge said, "all metaphors are grounded on an apparent likeness of things essentially different."[16] "Essentially" makes a problem. The two theories could easily be merged into one, since there must be some degree of resemblance if a substitution is to be possible. But even if the merger is not effected, metaphor is a cognitive act, or at least it may be, a device to make further experience possible. But this is problematic. Metaphors can't establish anything. They conspire with the mind in its enjoyment of freedom, but they can't demonstrate that anything is the case. How then can they be cognitive? At best, they are a suggestive figure, helpful in organizing experience, but they can't show that an order of experience has indeed been established. The mood of a metaphor is subjunctive or optative, never indicative. There is another problem. Only some parts of a metaphor are likely to be activated. If a metaphor is a suggested relation between the thing meant and the further thing said—between the tenor and the vehicle—the relation activates only those parts of the vehicle that are resonant with the tenor. A. W. Schlegel had a more buoyant view: "Strictly speaking, a metaphor can never be too bold. All things stand in relation to one another, and every thing therefore signifies every other thing, each part of the universe mirrors the whole: these are just as much philosophic as poetic truths."[17] But these attitudes are not contradictory. No matter how bold a metaphor is, it has to be interpreted, and the interpretation brings into life—activates, I would say—only those parts of it that tell; you don't heed the bits that fly off on their own. Why some parts reso-

nate and others don't is a hard question. The answer is probably to
be found among the cultural conditions. One of the many problems with the substitution theory, considered by itself, is that—as
Paul Ricoeur notes—"if the metaphorical term is really a substituted term, it carries no new information, since the absent term
(if one exists) can be brought back in; and if there is no information conveyed, then metaphor has only an ornamental, deco-
rative value."[18]

To see a likeness in things that are essentially different requires
an act of judgment. Aristotle values it supremely for that reason.
Indeed, his respect for such a capacity lets him put up with the
deficiencies of metaphor in other respects. In fact, he distrusted
metaphors; he thought them flighty things. They should be kept
under observation, reduced to the status of occasional ornaments.
They can raise one's style, but they present a risk while trying to
raise it. They must be curbed by the use of standard words in a style
mainly denotative and rational. Ordinary usage keeps the style decent. Every now and again you may guard your style against
meanness by resorting to metaphors for embellishment, but moderation is everything. Aristotle hasn't quite made up his mind
whether metaphors are a good thing or not. Questionably good,
in strict moderation, he seems to settle for. A rational style, using
mostly standard words that refer to standard things, is the best
practice. Aristotle was a philosopher, determined to protect his
calling. He thought of metaphors as functions of naming: the
name of something is transferred to something else. The transfer
is justified by its discovering likeness in things apparently dissimi-
lar. He maintained the conviction that a thing has a "proper"
name, sanctioned by social convention. I can report that I'm raising
a glass of red wine, because every word in that sentence, including

"a" and "of," is sustained by conventions operative in the English-speaking tribe to which I belong, every word, and the standard interpretation of a sentence. It is necessary to retain the privilege of "the proper" meaning because, without it, there would be no way of maintaining the "is not" within what Ricoeur calls "the ontological vehemence of the (metaphorical) 'is.'"[19] "The ship ploughs the waves": we deal sufficiently with this metaphor by saying, "Well, no, it doesn't, but I grant that in a fairly loose sense it does." Aristotle was normally rather grim about this. What he mostly demanded of metaphor was that it keep out of his way. He would not have been pleased to consider the relation of metaphor to possible worlds, utopias, dystopias, revolution, hypothetical structures entirely dependent on the creative imagination. He never forgot the logic he invented.

It is strange, then, that, abandoning common sense for once, he enthuses about metaphor and calls it the one indubitable sign of genius, the ability to see similarity in dissimilarity. How is this such a transcendent gift of nature that it can't be learned? Aristotle's sentence about metaphor and genius leaves off, almost as if he were afraid he had gone too far. The obvious contrast is with Longinus, who is so passionately given to the sublime that he keeps on telling you to grasp instances of it now in Demosthenes, now in Thucydides, now in Herodotus, as if some stroke of it must convince you to feel the blow. Aristotle's praise of Homer for presenting things as actions, giving life to lifeless things, is more far-reaching than the brief note allows for—surprising, since Aristotle's sense of tragedy and epic was predicated on motive and action. He may have thought that he didn't need a lecture note to prompt him to say things that were already second nature to him.

If Aristotle felt queasy about metaphor, it was, I think, because he felt much the same about imagination. The main evidence for this is the Third Book of his treatise on the soul, *De Anima*. He starts off with the standard view that "imagination is the faculty in virtue of which we say that an image presents itself to us, and if we exclude the metaphorical use of the term, it is some one of the faculties or habits in virtue of which we judge, and judge truly or falsely."[20] The metaphorical occasion seems to arise when we use the word interchangeably to say "Yes, I see" and "It seems to be the case." The word "image" in this sentence is not as clear as I'd like it to be. Aristotle generally uses φαντασία to mean "mental image." The Loeb editor W. S. Hett says that the imagination has two senses in Aristotle: sometimes "it operates in the presence of the sensible object and thus 'interprets' the object to the mind; and sometimes it operates in the absence of the sensible object, and then is either a form of memory or what we call 'pure imagination.' "[21] I'm not sure what we call "pure imagination," unless it is the spontaneous production of images, apparently from nowhere. However, I've met a strong argument that in this particular case (*De Anima*, 3.428a1) Aristotle means nothing as forthright as "mental image" but something closer to semblance, guise, or even apparition.[22] This would be in accord with the Loeb editor's second sense of imagination, where there are no sensory images; it would also meet Aristotle's troubled preoccupation, in this section, with imagination in its relation to dreams, sleep, hallucinations, and closed eyes. He insists that while imagination is in some way involved in perception and judgment, "imaginings prove for the most part false" (428a12). I think the trouble with imagination, according to Aristotle, is that its deliverances don't meet the criteria of true judgment. There is something dubious about them, as there is about metaphors.

Aristotle was the first philosopher of language to announce a distinction between the literal and the metaphorical. He had to do this because he found metaphors rampant in Homer, Plato, and Empedocles. He felt awkward about metaphors because he thought they were obscure and therefore a nuisance when the demonstration of a truth was necessary. Besides, he was confident, as G. E. R. Lloyd has noted, "that literal truth was there to be attained, and while that was usually, no doubt, a sign of a certain simplistic overconfidence on his part, it provided, we may be sure, a powerful incentive to the pursuit of his style of scientific investigation."[23] He would have brushed aside any modern claims that language as such is metaphorical, just as he took it for granted that there is a valid distinction between the normal or proper word for a thing, authenticated by common usage, and a strange or far-fetched word, though this metaphorical word was justified where an esoteric resemblance had to be admitted. Normally, the tenor is a poor, famished signifier, characterized by lack. The vehicle is an irresponsible signifier, characterized by excess.

I'll offer two examples of the ability to see likeness between things essentially different. In *The Winter's Tale* Leontes, already mad with sexual jealousy, chides Hermione for having kept him on the hook for quite a while before saying yes:

> Why, that was when
> Three crabbed months had soured themselves to death
> Ere I could make thee open thy white hand
> And clap thyself my love. (I.ii.101–104)

"Crabbed" and "soured" suggest crab apples getting so sour that they can't be eaten at all. Leontes is still sore about the delay. The metaphor is good because the apples have enough likeness to Leontes's resentment, but the likeness isn't obvious; it takes a minute's

thought to see it. The vehicle is excessive because it takes possession of the discourse and makes argument about it impossible.

Donne's speaker in "The Ecstasy" is getting tired of giving the
woman high-minded reasons for making love. He is ready to say,
"To our bodies turn we then":

> So must pure lovers' souls descend
> > T'affections, and to faculties,
> Which sense may reach and apprehend,
> > Else a great prince in prison lies.

A. J. Smith makes the standard comment:

> A great prince exercises his power over his realm through his
> officers who are his eyes, ears and arms; and a prince in prison,
> unable to make contact with the world, loses the effective na-
> ture of a prince. So the lovers, however pure and perfect their
> union of souls, would lose the effective nature of love did not
> their oneness activate itself in the union of bodies.[24]

I have always thought the great prince is the speaker's erect penis,
imprisoned in his clothes. Either way, there is enough likeness to
hold the parts of the metaphor together. Aristotle would have con-
sented. The likeness in "a great prince" is itself high and mighty.

I have never seen it remarked that you could have a distinction
between slow and quick metaphors. Most metaphors are quick;
they get from tenor to vehicle in a leap as if they already knew
their mind. A slow metaphor gives an impression of the mind
sorting things out, or moving as if by chance and luck among
feelings that are seen to resemble one another only in retrospect
The most beautiful slow metaphor I know is in Beckett's *Worstward*

Ho: "Nothing and yet a woman. Old and yet old. On unseen knees. Stooped as loving memory some old gravestones stoop. In that old graveyard. Names gone and when to when. Stoop mute over the graves of none."[25] The tenor is woman, the vehicle gravestone. Beckett makes his slow way from one to the other by murmuring "old . . . old . . . old . . . old," by recalling the "In Loving Memory" of gravestones that have outlived the names they undertook to remember, by repeating the "Stooped . . . stoop" that embraces woman and gravestone. Names gone and when to when, date of birth to date of death. The whole is enacted in the slow cortège of "Stoop mute over the graves of none."

There is also "extended metaphor," as I might call it, where the figurative work is done not just by a word but by a larger trans-port from one style to another. This is usually noted in discus-sions of the "free indirect style," where a narrative passage starts in the third-person and at some point veers to acknowledge the character in the case by using the words or phrases she would use if she were in charge of her own story. Here is the beginning of George Saunders's "The Barber's Unhappiness":

> Mornings the barber left his stylists inside and sat out front of his shop, drinking coffee and ogling every woman in sight. He ogled old women and pregnant women and women whose photographs were passing on the sides of buses and, this morn-ing, a woman with close-cropped black hair and tear-stained cheeks, who wouldn't be half bad if she'd just make an effort, clean up her face a little and invest in some decent clothes, some white tights and a short skirt maybe, knee boots and a cowboy hat and a cigarillo, say, and he pictured her kneeling

on a crude Mexican sofa, in a little mud hut, daring him to take her, and soon they'd screwed their way into some sort of bean-field while some gaucho guys played soft guitars, although actually he'd better put the gaucho guys behind some trees or a rock wall so they wouldn't get all hot and bothered from watching the screwing and swoop down and stab him and have their way with Miss Hacienda as he bled to death.[26]

One sentence: third-person narration down to "tear-stained cheeks" and again four words, "and he pictured her" perhaps to show that the narrator hasn't entirely resigned. But the rest is "free indirect style," where the story is handed over to the barber to let him express himself, run with his fantasy. Considered as style, it is indeed free and indirect, free because it gives the character his freedom, indirect because it doesn't present the story—this part of it anyway—with the authority of an independent narrator. Considered as rhetoric, it is an extended metaphor, I would say, the tenor down to the tear-stained cheeks, all the rest—except for "and he pictured her" (a blemish, I think)—the vehicle. As often happens, the vehicle is far more interesting than the tenor, as excess is livelier than lack; it's the place where we come to the supreme value of a metaphor, that it gives us more abundant life.

Three figures often referred to together—metonymy, simile, and metaphor—are alike in at least one respect: led by any one of them, you are instructed to think of a particular thing or class of thing and then, a split second later, to think of another particular thing or class of thing. Thinking of the second thing, you are urged to hold the first one in your mind and to think of the two simultaneously, or as near simultaneously as you can manage, "two thinks at a time," as Joyce says in *Finnegans Wake* (583.7). Why you are so instructed is a question. It may be that the ability to hold two things—two images, say—simultaneously in one's mind and to weigh some relation between them marks an advanced stage of civilization, like dancing or juggling. But there may be a price—a small one, probably—to be paid. Gaston Bachelard says, in *The Poetics of Reverie*, that "any comparison diminishes the expressive qualities of the terms of the comparison."[27] I think he means that a comparison holds the terms in their character, refuses to allow them to spread their wings. "The word 'inspiration' is too general to express the originality of inspired words." Bachelard is also expounding the resources of reverie, an attribute of the poetic imagination exempt from rational economies.

Metonymy is a figure of contiguity and causation: something happens to be close to something else that is relevant to the occasion, or it is close to it for a producible reason. In metonymy "the fact intended to be expressed is denoted by one of [its] adjuncts" (OED). It is mentioned to make the reference more elaborate, touching on a wider range of implication. Aeneas, avenging himself on Turnus for the killing of Pallas, says: "Pallas te hoc vulnere, Pallas / immolat" (*Aeneid*, 12.948–9). "With this wound Pallas, Pallas, makes you his sacrificial offering." Michael Silk has commented on these lines:

> If you are faced with a deviant usage wherein each word is *literally* possible in an expanded context in a sense approximating to that of its given use, you have metonymy . . . "Pallas" might be expanded to "I, Aeneas, on behalf of Pallas," and "wound" to "this weapon which I, Aeneas, am holding,

through which I am in the process of, or am just on the point of, inflicting a wound" . . . The absent Pallas is "there" in the weapon's stroke to avenge his own wound and Aeneas's too.[28]

(A deviant usage is one that veers from standard words, words—as Aristotle said in the *Poetics*—that are "used by a community.") Roman Jakobson has compared the differences between metonymy and metaphor to certain differences in aphasic disorders. He has also referred to the relation between metonymy (or synecdoche, which he treats as much the same) and realism in the novel:

> Following the path of contiguous relationships, the Realist author metonymically digresses from the plot to the atmosphere and from the characters to the setting in space and time. He is fond of synecdochic details. In the scene of Anna Karenina's suicide Tolstoy's artistic attention is focused on the heroine's handbag; and in *War and Peace* the synecdoches "hair on the upper lip" and "bare shoulders" are used by the same writer to stand for the female characters to whom these features belong.[29]

The effect of verisimilitude is gained mostly by metonymy, which puts things together that you would expect to find together in the first place—but you don't count on it—and that you are pleased to find together when the novelist has put them there. Together, they gratify one's sense of reality, the ways things are. In *Metaphors We Live By,* George Lakoff and Mark Johnson give many examples of metonymy in ordinary life. Most of them involve a kind of shorthand, as when one entity is used to refer to another that is often found beside it. They list many of these under various categories: the part for the whole, producer for product, object used for user, controller for controlled, institution for the people responsible—"Exxon has raised its prices again"—the place for the institution, the building for the event—"Watergate changed our politics."[30] The difference between metonyms and metaphors is that metonyms appeal to what we already know. That's why social shorthand is possible. If someone says, "We need some new faces around here," we know he doesn't mean faces; he means new people.

A simile is a figure of likeness: one thing is said to be like something else. Why this is worth saying is a further question, answerable differently on each occasion, subject to the reflection that likeness and difference is one of the few foundational categories of thought. In a simile, the things compared are not altered by the comparison, though after reading or hearing the simile you may think of the things differently or afresh:

> black, naked women with necks
> wound round and round with wire
> like the necks of light bulbs.[31]

The first necks are literal; the second, figurative. You may think differently of the necks of certain black, naked women in future, or differently of the necks of light bulbs, but you will not think that any of these is really changed by your attention. Your thought is local and possibly tenable, for the time being. In saying that something is like something else, you try to be straightforward, as literal as possible. By "literal" I mean the primary sense of a word, *verbum proprium* privileged by common usage. No wild intention transpires in a language that says that something is like something else. In English, as in Elizabeth Bishop's English above, the word "like"—or some such word as "as"—testifies to the simile's modest ambition. It has a job to do, and it does it: it proposes a comparison between two entities, in one particular respect, or at most in a few respects. "O my Luve's like a red, red rose / That's newly sprung in June" in one grand respect. She is not a rose, but she is like an ideal rose; if she has thorns, I don't mention them, and I hope she will not fade after a few days. The simile sets a limit to the comparison. But when the queen, in Shakespeare's *Richard II,* sees her husband, the deposed, defeated, one-time king, walking toward Pomfret, and whispers to herself

> But soft, but see, or rather do not see
> My fair rose wither. Yet look up, behold,
> That you in pity may dissolve to dew
> And wash him fresh again with true-love tears (V.i.6–9)

she may be thought to speak "my fair rose" as a metaphor, exempt from limitation—identity, not mere resemblance—and then to let her voice drop further into the abjection of "wither." "As quiet as a mouse," no other quality of mice being invoked. In a simile, each of the constituents holds its character; nothing is changed:

> Let us go then, you and I,
> When the evening is spread out against the sky
> Like a patient etherized upon a table.[32]

Maybe the relation between evening and sky is changed in your mind, but not forever: you will go on to the next evening and take it more-or-less as before. At most, Eliot's lines will cause a flurry in your mind for as long as they are there. They tell you something about Prufrock's mind, and only later about yours.

This also applies to epic similes, as we call them, mainly because Homer, Virgil, Dante, and Milton often used them. In the first book of Milton's *Paradise Lost* Satan approaches his angels, lying distraught on the burning lake:

> Nathless he so endured, till on the beach
>
> Of that inflamèd sea, he stood and called
>
> His legions, angel forms, who lay entranced
>
> Thick as autumnal leaves that strow the brooks
>
> In Vallombrosa, where th' Etrurian shades
>
> High overarched embow'r; or scattered sedge
>
> Afloat, when with fierce winds Orion armed
>
> Hath vexed the Red Sea coast, whose waves o'erthrew
>
> Busiris and his Memphian chivalry,
>
> While with perfidious hatred they pursued
>
> The sojourners of Goshen, who beheld
>
> From the safe shore their floating carcasses
>
> And broken chariot wheels. So thick bestrown
>
> Abject and lost lay these, covering the flood,
>
> Under amazement of their hideous change. (I.299–313)

These lines invite a comment from musical criticism. Between one "thick" and another, ten lines later, we have a series of similes, a cadenza during which the narrative stops, to start again with "He called so loud, that all the hollow deep / Of hell resounded." The soft rhyme of "loud" and "resounded" enacts what it says. The angelic forms, "thick as autumnal leaves," are not numbered by the similes; they are only as vast as we choose to imagine them. The similes provide a breathing space in the narrative. But you can do more than breathe in a breathing space. You can wonder, if only for a moment, whether the "angel forms" are Israelites or Egyptians, a question not quite resolved till "the sojourners of Goshen." You can wonder—wonder being the main allowance here—what it means for angels to be "entranced," a state clear enough only in humans, and whether the angels have any quality but number until we are told, ten lines later, that they are "abject and lost." You would even wonder whether Homer and Virgil are still in the context. Stanley Fish's comment is apposite: "A simile, especially an epic simile, is an attempt to place persons and/or things, perceived in *a* time and *a* space, in the larger perspective from which their significance must finally be determined."[33] But "the larger perspective" is not as specific as the "the" implies: it is anything that is reasonably called into the reader's mind while these words, these sentences, are going on, anything consistent with what Fish calls, a page earlier, "the awe that attends incomprehensibility." Mostly what the similes say is that there are vastnesses closer to home than Satan's cohorts. But the "or," in "or scattered sedge," is permissive, it gives you leave to be distracted from the main subject and not to be restlessly waiting for its resumption.

In *The Waves,* Louis thinks of Rhoda, in the schoolroom, staring at the blackboard: "Her shoulder-blades meet across her back like the wings of a small butterfly."[34] That sentence doesn't just compare Rhoda's shoulder blades to the wings of a small butterfly; it compares Louis's feeling about Rhoda to his appreciation of small butterflies—which is likely to include his feeling for their beauty, their vulnerability, fragility, the certainty that their lives will be short. Rhoda's shoulder blades, remembered with devotion, are the occasion of the feeling. The feeling is not trivial, even though it is given to us without the freight of Homer and Virgil. This, we are meant to infer, is the way educated, upper-middle-class men are likely to respond to the meeting of a girl's shoulder blades across her back.

Keats's "On Seeing the Elgin Marbles" begins:

My spirit is too weak—mortality
Weighs heavily on me like unwilling sleep,
And each imagined pinnacle and steep
Of godlike hardship tells me I must die
Like a sick eagle looking at the sky.[35]

The metaphors are: "spirit," "weighs," "pinnacle," and "steep."
The similes are: "unwilling sleep," "godlike," and the last line. "My
spirit is too weak." Too weak to endure, it is "like a sick eagle"—a
prince among birds—"looking at the sky." The two parts of the
statement remain unchanged by their relation; there is no blur,
nor is there "interinanimation."

Still, a simile is often such a minor act of imagination that
some readers have wondered whether or not it is worth the bother.
Hegel's first thought was that it was idle repetition, a wearisome
superfluity, "since the meaning is explicitly present already and
needs no further mode of configuration to make it intelligible."
He nearly answers the question why are you making similes? by
saying, "because I can." He doesn't accept that a simile is justified
by its giving greater vivacity to the expression or that it makes the
thing meant clearer:

> The proper aim of the simile we must therefore find in the
> poet's subjective imagination. However clearly he makes him-
> self aware of the subject-matter which he intends to express,
> however far he has brought this subject home to his mind in
> its more abstract universality and has expressed it [to himself]
> in this universality, still he finds himself equally driven to
> seek a concrete shape for the subject and to make perceptible
> to himself in a sensuous appearance the meaning already be-
> fore his mind.[36]

By "a labour of the spirit," the poet attaches to the given topic "a world of heterogeneous phenomena." That is at the root of a simile.

Hegel continued to think that poets make similes and draw comparisons for the pleasure of exercising their imaginations. But gradually he found other reasons too. One was that "similes are a dwelling on one and the same topic, which thereby is made the substantial centre of a series of other ideas remote from it; through their indication or portrayal the greater interest in the topic compared becomes objective." Such dwelling shows "a feeling immersing itself in what it feels," often to the degree of absurdity, it must be admitted. But the merit of the epic simile, as in the *Iliad,* is that by holding the comparisons to one topic, the poet raises us above our immediate, practical interest in it—our curiosity, expectation, hope, fear, our engagement with cause and consequence—and presents us with pictures "like works of sculpture, peaceful and plastic, designed for *theoretical* consideration." In Shakespearean tragedy, as Hegel says, it is a mark of the hero that even in the midst of his grief he can maintain sufficient freedom "to occupy himself with some far-off idea and in this remote object to express his own fate to himself in an image." Even Richard II, when he realizes that Henry must have the crown, says:

> Give me the crown. Here, cousin, seize the crown;
> Here, cousin;
> On this side my hand, and on that yours.
> Now is this golden crown like a deep well
> That owes two buckets, filling one another,
> The emptier ever dancing in the air,
> The other down, unseen and full of water:

> That bucket down and full of tears am I,
>
> Drinking my griefs, whilst you mount up on high. (*Richard II,*
>
>   IV.i.181–189)

The first two lines are mockery, the repetition of "crown" and "cousin" the sort of thing you would say to a child. Simile is the form of Richard's freedom, slight as that otherwise is. He can at his weakest think gorgeously of an empty bucket "dancing in the air." The metaphor—"Drinking my griefs"—contrasts with Bolingbroke's airy freedom; he doesn't need any such sustenance.

In the *Rhetoric,* Aristotle held that there is little difference between simile and metaphor: "When the poet says 'He rushed as a lion,' it is a simile, but 'The lion rushed' [with *lion* referring to a man] would be a metaphor. . . . Similes are metaphors needing an explanatory word."[37]

That is still a fairly common view: some readers hold that metaphor is really a kind of simile, others that simile is really a kind of metaphor. John Middleton Murry claimed that "metaphor is compressed simile."[38] He then quoted a short passage from Katherine Mansfield's *Six Years After:* "Far out, as though idly, listlessly, gulls were flying. Now they settled on the waves, now they beat up into the rainy air *and shone against the pale sky like the lights within a pearl.*" The words he italicized, he said, "would be called indifferently an image or a simile." Change them to "shining lights in the pale pearl of sky," he continued, and it becomes a metaphor. But "the act of creative perception remains the same."[39] In fact it doesn't. There is the redundancy of "shining lights." Mansfield's version keeps "shone" at a decent distance from "lights," and "pale sky" from "pearl," as is proper to a simile. Murry's "pale pearl of sky" is a metaphorical equivocation resolved by the banal answer "of sky." Mansfield's "like" doesn't claim more than it should, the comparison being justly partial. There is no reason to maintain that the acts of creative perception are the same. In the event, having said that there is no difference between simile and metaphor, Murry went on to treat them as at least circumstantially different, found in different places, prose and poetry, having different qualities of decorum and audacity. Quoting Cleopatra's celebration of the dead Antony, Murry had no doubt that the splendor of it moved rapidly between simile and metaphor, a movement proper to Cleopatra's invocation of Antony as a great force of nature:

> His legs bestrid the ocean; his reared arm
> Crested the world; his voice was propertied
> As all the tuned spheres, and that to friends;
> But when he meant to quail and shake the orb,
> He was as rattling thunder. For his bounty,
> There was no winter in't: an Antony it was
> That grew the more by reaping. His delights
> Were dolphinlike, they showed his back above
> The element they lived in. In his livery
> Walked crowns and crownets; realms and islands were
> As plates dropped from his pocket. (Shakespeare, *Antony and Cleopatra,* V.ii.83–93)

"Bestrid," "Crested," and "propertied" are metaphors. "As rattling thunder" is a simile. "No winter": metaphor. "Grew the more by reaping": metaphor. "Dolphinlike": simile, but the coda—"showed his back above / The element they lived in"—enhances the simile almost to the degree of metaphor. "Walked crowns and crownets": metaphor. "As plates": simile, again enhanced by "dropped from his pocket."

Hegel, taking his bearings from Aristotle's *Poetics,* held that there was small difference between metaphor and simile, except that metaphor accommodated more elaborate and daring vivacities:

> Metaphor may arise from the wit of a subjective caprice which, to escape from the commonplace, surrenders to a piquant impulse, not satisfied until it has succeeded in finding related traits in the apparently most heterogeneous material and therefore, to our astonishment, combining things that are poles apart from one another.[40]

Doubtful about the merit of personification, Hegel was content with the milder forms of metaphor, but he insisted that, like simile, they should transfer "the phenomena, activities, and situations of a higher sphere to the content of lower areas" and present "meanings of this more subordinate kind in the shape and picture of the loftier ones." He was evidently pleased to make this concession:

> In this sense it is quite common for us to speak of "*laughing* fields," "*angry* flood," or to say with Calderón "the waves *sigh* under the heavy burden of the ships." What is solely human is used here as an expression for the natural. Roman poets too used this sort of metaphor, as for example Virgil (*Georgics,* iii.132) says: "Cum graviter tunsis gemit area frugibus" [when the threshing floor *groans* heavily under the threshing of the corn].[41]

But he thought that metaphor incited a lot of hocus-pocus, even sometimes in Shakespeare.

There is often too a slippage between metonymy and metaphor, or a deliberate equivocation. Conrad makes good use of this in *Lord Jim.* He contrives, by a bizarre device, that Marlow should meet Jim during the court of inquiry into the debacle of the *Patna.*

A crowd of villagers comes into the court for another case. A yellow dog has followed them in, as Marlow reports, "weaving himself in and out amongst people's legs in that mute stealthy way native dogs have." Marlow's companion stumbles over the dog, and he says to Marlow, "Look at that wretched cur." Jim, who is walking ahead, thinks the remark refers to him, and he spins round to accost Marlow: "Did you speak to me?" Marlow answers "No," and more elaborately, "As far as I know, I haven't opened my lips in your hearing." Jim doesn't believe him: "Who's a cur now—hey?" Marlow points at the dog: " 'Nobody dreamt of insulting you,' I said." "He contemplated the wretched animal, that moved no more than an effigy: it sat with ears pricked and its sharp muzzle pointed into the doorway, and suddenly snapped at a fly like a piece of mechanism."

At last, Jim concedes the point: "Altogether my mistake . . . You may well forgive me." Marlow invites him to dine with him at the Malabar House. The conversation, such as it is, continues, but the word "cur," now a metaphor, lodges itself in Jim's speech: " 'Do you know what *you* would have done? Do you? And you don't think yourself' . . . he gulped something . . . 'you don't think yourself a—a—cur?' " A few pages later: "You think me a cur for standing there, but what would you have done?"[42]

The yellow dog is a metonym, to begin with. We may not expect to find him in the courthouse, but his coming along there with the villagers is not surprising. As a figure of contiguity, he is satisfactory. When Jim admits his mistake, he doesn't remove the word "cur" from his vocabulary; it sticks to his mind as a common metaphor, he can't let it go.

The better tradition of commentary on metaphor maintains that it differs from simile if only because—as Howard Nemerov put it—"the simile isolates for you the likeness in virtue of which the comparison is made; the metaphor leaves it up to you to isolate the likeness or for that matter not to isolate it." The metaphor "doesn't give itself away, but awaits, if it doesn't indeed demand, the reader's participation for its fulfillment."[43] But a distinguishing mark of metaphor is that, pressing beyond similarity among dissimilarities, it takes the risk of identifying the two disparate entities. In metaphor, we are tempted to say that A is B, but we hold back from that assertion. As Northrop Frye says: "In metaphors of the type 'A is B,' the 'is' is not really a predicate at all. The real function of the 'is' in 'Joseph is a fruitful bough' is to annihilate the space between the 'Joseph' who is there, on our left as it were, and the 'bough' which is there on our right, and place them in a world where everything is 'here.' "[44] I would say that the fruitful bough is there as soon as we think of it, but not before. We are engaging in a metaphor when we see, or think we see, or propose to see, one thing in the light of another; it is an instance of perspective, not necessarily of resemblance. But the relative status of each member of the metaphor is an issue. In the Christian tradition, as we have seen, with Tertullian as exemplar, the vehicle does not replace the tenor or indeed overwhelm it: what has existed still exists, in a mind generous enough to respect both. Even a relation of "figure" to "fulfillment," in Auerbach's terms, does not erase the figure. Feeling may run both ways, even though "fulfillment" is deemed to have completed a fateful sequence. In reading a metaphor, there is nothing to prevent us from going back on our tracks rather than sticking to the apparent official direction. This raises the possibility that while a metaphor is a double entity, the duality might be turned into a higher, richer unity, though theorists of metaphor have had little success in showing how this might be done. Some scholars, as we have seen, speak of "fusion" of the members. Richards refers to the cooperation, the copresence of tenor and vehicle.[45] None of these implies that a resolution is to be sought on a higher level than that of the interaction of tenor and vehicle. Hegel seemed to think it might be.

In some metaphors, the vehicle is so much more engrossing than the tenor that we search for the tenor and don't find it till we have seen the vehicle run its course. Shakespeare's Sonnet 73 begins:

> That time of year thou mayst in me behold,
> When yellow leaves, or none, or few, do hang
> Upon those boughs which shake against the cold,
> Bare ruined choirs, where late the sweet birds sang.[46]

On first reading, we find ten words passing before we have any notion of what's the matter. More: how can we behold a time? The first line tells us nothing about the tenor, only with the yellow leaves do we begin to intuit the condition the speaker is attributing to himself: "hang," "shake," and "cold" do the remaining work. The state itself is not named, but we have enough evidence to deduce it. Even in four short lines, the poet takes every opportunity of using each reference as a means of escape from itself: "yellow leaves" yield to "none," then to a revisionary "few"—a peculiar sequence—then to "bare ruined choirs" which can't avoid bringing up a picture of the choir stalls where boys in monasteries sang before Henry VIII despoiled those sanctities. The words of the vehicle are strung out along a line of different vicissitudes, issuing from the misery of getting old.

In metaphor, the two constituents of the figure are related interactively: "reciprocally active; acting upon or influencing each other," as the OED has it. The great dictionary also refers to a computer, "that allows a two-way flow of information between it and a user." This is Donne's "interinanimation." As in "The Extasie":

> When love, with one another so
> Interinanimates two soules,
> That abler soule, which thence doth flow,
> Defects of lonelinesse controules.[47]

In *Principles of Literary Criticism,* Richards remembers Donne's word, but abbreviates it by a syllable: "Conflicts, resolutions and interanimations. . . ." In *The Philosophy of Rhetoric* he keeps to Donne's word.

Metaphor, more than simile or metonymy, expresses one's desire to be free, and to replace the given world by an imagined world of one's devising. So the first part of the metaphor, the tenor, is likely to be diminished or even dislodged by the vehicle as the interinanimation of the words proceeds. More than likeness is entailed; the process is audacious, close to identification of the two terms. Kenneth Burke refers to metaphor as a device by which we gain "perspective by incongruity," "extending the use of a term by taking it from the context in which it was habitually used and applying it to another."[48] As in Donne's "The Canonization":

> Call us what you will, wee are made such by love;
> > Call her one, mee another flye,
> We're Tapers, too, and at our owne cost die.[49]

The pitch of audacity is reached in "owne."

Sometimes a metaphor arises from a simile. In the last moments of Shakespeare's *Antony and Cleopatra* Caesar enters and, seeing Cleopatra dead but not quite believing that she is dead, says

but she looks like sleep,
As she would catch another Antony
In her strong toil of grace. (V.ii.348–350)

She looks like sleep: a simile. Then the simile is extended to become, through an erotic verb—"catch another Antony"—the tenor of a metaphor, fulfilled in the vehicle, "her strong toil of grace." The OED gives this line to illustrate one of the meanings of "toil," "a trap or snare for wild beasts." "Toil of grace"? I take it that Cleopatra's grace is the particular kind of snare she would set, not mere airs and graces but the whole range of beauty and glamour—strong indeed—that might be thought to be a gift of God.

In Ian McEwan's *Solar,* Michael Beard, on a professional trip to the Antarctic, falls on the snow while hoisting himself to the seat behind the guide on a snowmobile and feels "a terrible rending pain in his groin, a cracking and a parting, like a birth, like a glacier calving."[50] "Like a birth" is a simile, but "a glacier calving" is a metaphor even though it is also delivered by "like." Who would have thought of it? Heinrich Lausberg agrees with majority opinion since Aristotle that "a *similitudo* must exist between the metaphorical description and that which it describes": "In the Aristotelian system, the semantic relationships 'from one species to another species' and 'according to analogy' correspond to *similitudo*. Since the *similitude* knows no limits, all possibilities are open to the metaphor also."[51]

As I have noted, Aristotle is responsible for most of the thinking about metaphor, including those notions brought up by disagreeing with him. More daring philosophers might have started the whole subject along different lines. Vico for instance: suppose the

third edition of his *The New Science* (1744) had attracted the readers it deserved. It might have pointed the question of metaphor in
other directions. Some readers might have thrown the book away,
dismayed by the speculative (but not specious) mythology that
occupied its first section, its presentation of the history of the human race as that of three ages:

> (1) the age of the gods in which the gentiles believed they lived
> under divine governments, and everything was commanded
> them by auspices and oracles, which are the oldest institutions
> in profane history, (2) the age of the heroes, in which they
> reigned everywhere in aristocratic commonwealths, on account
> of a certain superiority of nature which they held themselves
> to have over the plebs, (3) the age of men, in which all men
> recognized themselves as equal in human nature, and there-
> fore they established first the popular commonwealths and
> then the monarchies, both of which are forms of human
> government.[52]

Corresponding to these three ages, there were three languages:

> (1) a mute language of signs and physical objects having natu-
> ral relations to the ideas they wished to express, (2) a language
> spoken by means of heroic emblems, or similitudes, compari-
> sons, images, metaphors, and natural descriptions, which make
> up the great body of the heroic language which was spoken at
> the time the heroes reigned, and (3) human language using
> words agreed upon by the people, a language of which they
> are absolute lords, and which is proper to the popular com-
> monwealths and monarchical states; a language whereby the

people may fix the meaning of the laws by which the nobles as well as the plebs are bound [section 320].

The first gentile peoples, "by a determined necessity of nature, were poets who spoke in poetic characters" (section 34). These characters "were certain imaginative genera (images for the most part of animate substances, of gods or heroes, formed by their imagination) to which they reduced all the species or all the particulars appertaining to each genus; exactly as the fables of human times" (section 34). If the first language was poetic and figurative, and the decorum of prose a later invention, it follows that the language of metaphor is not a deviation from literal language; literal language is the economy practiced on metaphor. The four master tropes are metaphor, metonymy, synecdoche, and irony:

> The most luminous and therefore the most necessary is metaphor. It is most praised when it gives sense and passion to insensate things, in accordance with the metaphysics already discussed (section 402), by which the first poets attributed to bodies the being of animate substances, with capacities measured by their own, namely sense and passion, and in this way made fables of them. Thus every metaphor so formed is a fable in brief (section 404). So, too, in general, metaphor makes up the great body of the language among all nations (section 444).

In all languages, according to Vico, "the greater part of the expressions relating to inanimate things are formed by metaphor from the human body and its parts and from the human senses and passions." Thus: the *brow* of a hill, the *eye* of a needle, the *lip* of a cup, and so on. But metaphor is not dependent on discovering similarity in dissimilarities; the metaphorical intellect, Vico says in *De nostri temporis studiorum ratione* (1708), puts new things in relation, to generate knowledge.[53] As for Vico's metonymy, synecdoche, and irony, the first poets "had to give names to things from the most particular and the most sensible ideas":

> Such ideas are the sources, respectively, of synecdoche and metonymy. Metonymy of agent for act resulted from the fact that names for agents were commoner than names for acts. Metonymy of subject for form and accident was due to inability to abstract forms and qualities from subjects. . . . Synecdoche developed into metaphor as particulars were elevated into universals, or parts united with the other parts together with which they make up their wholes. . . . The use of "head" for man or person, so frequent in vulgar Latin, was due to the fact that in the forests only the head of a man could be seen from a distance. Irony certainly could not have begun until the period of reflection, because it is fashioned of falsehood by dint of a reflection which wears the mask of truth. (section 408)

But all these tropes issued from "a wholly corporeal imagination," as Vico calls it, an imagination engaged with the things that surround it. "Imagination is more robust in proportion as reasoning power is weak" (section 185). The first people created things according to their own ideas:

> But this creation was infinitely different from that of God. For God, in his purest intelligence, knows things, and, by knowing them, creates them; but they, in their robust ignorance, did it by virtue of a wholly corporeal imagination. And

because it was quite corporeal, they did it with marvelous sublimity; a sublimity such and so great that it excessively perturbed the very persons who by imagining did the creating, for which they were called "poets," which is Greek for "creators" (section 376).

The reference to "sublimity" brings together Longinus, Vico, and Edmund Burke among many other adepts of that experience. It also indicates a tradition of commentary on metaphor not hostile to Aristotle but standing somewhat apart from him.

The minimal requirement in a metaphor is that the tenor is changed by the vehicle; not replaced by it or superseded but changed in quality or character by the new company it is made to keep. In extreme cases the change is revolutionary; it issues in a possible world, proclaimed by the audacity of the metaphor. The metaphor declares its independence. Readers then decide whether or not the declaration is justified by the enlightenment it announces. Sometimes, as we have seen and will see again, the idiom of tenor and vehicle doesn't apply, or doesn't apply very well, especially where the issues are not to be found in the external world and we have to look for authority to the only authority that remains: the apprehensive power of the mind, the particular mind in the case.

No Resemblance

"Like" and "like" and "like"—but what is the thing
that lies beneath the semblance of the thing?

—Virginia Woolf

*M*rs. Riordan's Protestant neighbors were justified in asking, of the Litany of the Blessed Virgin, "How could a woman be a tower of ivory or a house of gold," but they were wrong to assume that the question was decisive.[1] They had read too many nineteenth-century realist novels. Empson's understanding of language was more generous. Commenting on two lines from Arthur Waley's Chinese translations—

Swiftly the years, beyond recall.
Solemn the stillness of this spring morning—

he remarked:

Lacking rhyme, metre, and any overt device such as comparison, these lines are what we should normally call poetry only by virtue of their compactness; two statements are made as if they were connected, and the reader is forced to consider their relations for himself. The reason why these facts should have been selected for a poem is left for him to invent; he will invent a variety of reasons and order them in his own mind. This, I think, is the essential fact about the poetical use of language.[2]

In *The Philosophy of Rhetoric* Richards quoted Empson's sentences with approval: they supported his understanding that the mind works by connecting things:

> Let us consider more closely what happens in the mind when we put together—in a sudden and striking fashion—two things belonging to very different orders of experience. The most important happenings—in addition to a general confused reverberation and strain—are the mind's efforts to connect them. The mind is a connecting organ, it works only by connecting and it can connect any two things in an indefinitely large number of different ways. Which of these it chooses is settled by reference to some larger whole or aim, and, though we may not discover its aim, the mind is never aimless. In all interpretation we are filling in connections, and for poetry, of course, our freedom to fill in—the absence of explicitly stated intermediate steps—is a main source of its powers.[3]

"Two things belonging to very different orders of experience": that sounds like the Aristotelian coordinates of metaphor. The reader has to invent reasons for their being put together: that sounds like the normal problem of reading a metaphor, and it makes the reader do most of the work. Readers will probably start by looking for a likeness, but if they are Mrs. Riordan's Protestants, they may not find one. If they are Catholics, they look for "some larger whole or aim" or they assume, without looking, that such a thing could be found. The individual invocations may not make sense—nobody wants to live in a tower of ivory or a house of gold—but the larger whole provides sense enough. Any invocation to the Blessed Virgin would do, provided it is supreme of its kind. Like any other conceit, it is not troubled by the charge that it's far-fetched; far-fetched is what it's supposed to be, a bold procession of hyperboles, given the speaker's feeling for the Virgin. The feeling brushes aside as petty any objections raised from a consideration of reason or taste. Empson makes the point that the poet Hood "uses puns to back away from the echoes and implications of words, to distract your attention by insisting on his ingenuity so that you can escape from sinking into the meaning."[4] For those of us in St. Peter's, Warrenpoint, who recited the Litany of the Blessed Virgin, probably had vague but sufficient confidence that our feeling for the Virgin was comprehensive enough to protect us from sinking into mere local meaning. We thought that Protestants were free to enjoy that trivial liberty.

Richards insists that metaphors are not restricted to resemblance, or at least not to resemblance pure and simple:

> We must not, with the 18th Century, suppose that the inter-actions of tenor and vehicle are to be confined to their resem-blances. There is disparity action too. When Hamlet uses the word *crawling*—
>
> > "What should such fellows as I do crawling between earth and heaven?"
> >
> > (Shakespeare, *Hamlet*, III.1.127–129)

—its force comes not only from whatever resemblances to vermin it brings in but at least equally from the differences that resist and control the influences of their resemblances. The implication there is that man should not so crawl. Thus, talk about the identification or fusion that a metaphor effects is nearly always misleading and pernicious. In general, there are very few metaphors in which disparities between tenor and vehicle are not as much operative as the similarities. Some similarity will commonly be the ostensive ground of the shift, but the peculiar modification of the tenor which the vehicle brings about is even more the work of their unlikenesses than of their likenesses.[5]

Still, Richards holds that metaphors begin with resemblance, but then disparities enforce themselves: the two values fight it out. This fight gives the metaphor the quality of struggle that Barthes looks for. It also allows that a metaphor has the ambition to change life by telling a different story about it. Richards assumes that tenor and vehicle refer to things out there in the world between which there is—or there may be found—a likeness of some sort: his metaphors are devices for administering the world afresh in the interest of the mind's freedom. His tenor and vehicle don't work when the entities invoked are not of this palpable world, when they are metaphysical, fantastic, the stuff of dreams and nightmares. I suppose, if *crawling* were to be used literally, as of a baby trying to exercise its arms and legs, Richards's disparities would not arise. Shakespeare's Sonnet 60 has these lines:

> Nativity, once in the main of light,
> Crawls to maturity, wherewith being crowned,

> Crookèd eclipses 'gainst his glory fight,
> And time that gave doth now his gift confound.

The most plausible way of reading these lines is to take "Nativity" to mean a new-born baby: "crawls" is enough justification. This is fine until "Crookèd eclipses" makes you think that it may mean "the astrological chart in which a person's destiny is mapped." The phrase I've just quoted comes from Stephen Booth's edition of the sonnets in which he gives four meanings of "Nativity": a new-born infant, the sun, the moment of birth considered in relation to astrological influences, and the astrological chart. The four meanings, he says, "come into and out of operation in response to the flow of contexts in the next eight lines."[6] It is doubtful that anyone could read in such a cluttered way. Most readers, if alert to the four meanings, would settle for one of them, probably the crawling child, and take the crooked eclipses to mean—as Booth allows it suggests—"the crookedness of an old man bent by age." Probably the effort to invent meanings and relations to justify the lines would cause the "general confused reverberation and strain" that Richards anticipated.

George Herbert's "Prayer (I)" is like the Litany of the Blessed Virgin in its processional or paratactic form, but it is a sonnet, fourteen lines in loose iambic pentametres, rhyming abab, cdcd, eff, ghh. There is only one tenor, the word "Prayer," and there are twenty-seven vehicles, nouns or noun-phrases in apposition to it: no main verbs. There are no connectives; the rhetorical figure by which the poem is impelled is asyndeton, where rapidity is achieved by removing connecting particles between one phrase or clause and the next. If the poem were written out as a litany, it would cause no scandal—one phrase is in loose apposition to the next, resemblance is not entailed:

> Prayer the Churches banquet, Angels age,
>> Gods breath in man returning to his birth,
>> The soul in paraphrase, heart in pilgrimage,
> The Christian plummet sounding heav'n and earth;
> Engine against th' Almightie, sinners tower,
>> Reversed thunder, Christ-side-piercing spear,
>> The six-daies world transposing in an houre,
> A kind of tune, which all things heare and fear;
> Softnesse, and peace, and joy, and love, and blisse,
>> Exalted Manna, gladnesse of the best,
>> Heaven in ordinarie, man well dressed,
> The milkie way, the bird of Paradise,
>> Church-bels beyond the starres heard, the souls
>> blood,
>> The land of spices; something understood.[7]

None of the vehicles is at all like the tenor. Each is a quality or power linked now to prayer, not already found there. The attributions are strange to the subject, free of likeness to it. This is a poem of the phrase, not of the clause: it has behind it not the form of the sentence, where syntax directs the force of mind from main clause through subordinate clauses. There is no subordination. Each paratactic item is independent of its companions; none of them is privileged. The metaphorical force of each phrase is designed to change the way we have thought about prayer and to have us live in that change, longer than for the moment. No syntactical articulation is needed. It is enough that the poet utters these phrases; he does not expect them to be refuted or even opposed.

Two stanzas of Vaughan's "The Night" have similar paratactic phrasing and similar metaphorical dartings:

> Dear night! this world's defeat;
>   The stop to busy fools; care's check and curb;
>   The day of Spirits; my soul's calm retreat
>   Which none disturb!
>   *Christ's* progress, and his prayer time;
>   The hours to which high Heaven doth chime.
>
>   God's silent, searching flight:
> When my Lord's head is filled with dew, and all
> His locks are wet with the clear drops of night;
>   His still, soft call;
>   His knocking time; the soul's dumb watch,
>   When Spirits their fair kindred catch.[8]

Donald Davie quoted these stanzas in *Articulate Energy: An Inquiry into the Syntax of English Poetry* to illustrate a mentality that "believes that significant action occurs outside the dimension of time ('reality' being 'timeless'), and that the significant acts of the mind, those by which it apprehends reality, are escapes out of time into eternity."[9] But he did not remark that each of Vaughan's metaphors would persuade its readers to assent to the values of this mentality. The procession of metaphors, in Vaughan's poem as in Herbert's, persuades by occupying the whole ground of the discourse, and by offering no alternatives.

Aristotle says in the *Poetics* (1459a7–8) that to devise a good metaphor is to see a likeness: "To gar eu metapherein to to homoion theōrein estin." Derrida has explicated the sentence: "Metaphor has always been defined as the trope of resemblance; not simply as the resemblance between a signifier and a signified but as the resemblance between two signs, one of which designates the other." Near the beginning of "Hyperion: A Fragment" Keats has this passage, a scene in which the "sad Goddess" tries to sustain the dethroned Saturn:

> As when, upon a tranced summer-night,
> Those green-rob'd senators of mighty woods,
> Tall oaks, branch-charmed by the earnest stars,
> Dream, and so dream all night without a stir,
> Save from one gradual solitary gust
> Which comes upon the silence, and dies off,
> As if the ebbing air had but one wave. . . .[10]

"Those green-rob'd senators" is a simple version of metaphor by resemblance, made possible by the shared green of the oaks and the near resemblance of "rob-d." "Senators" is obviously, in Aristotle's terms, an improper word drawn over from an implied, understood context where it would be proper. The metaphor says something new and strange about the oaks, and possibly about senators: it also draws across the landscape a human, lordly intimation.

Neither Aristotle nor Longinus seems to have considered the possibility that there might be metaphors that float free of resemblance. They could still be metaphors because they would transfer a word or a phrase from its standard place in the sentence to an "improper" one: that is the essential requirement. But they would not depend on a resemblance of one thing to another, an occult likeness between things essentially unlike, or a resemblance between two signs such as Derrida indicated. Aristotle, more strictly than Longinus, seems to have regarded likeness as the most helpful adjunct to the demonstration of truth. But he already felt so much doubt about metaphor that he saw no reason to incur more. The privilege of resemblance has rarely been questioned: it is a major resource in the sciences. Still, it is not a self-evident principle in considerations of metaphor. Hugo Friedrich maintains, in his study of the modern lyric, that Rimbaud's "Le Bateau ivre" is "an absolute metaphor throughout, speaking only of the boat and never of the symbolized 'I.'" The metaphor, "no longer a mere figure of comparison, now creates an identity." I'm not sure what he means by "creates an identity" or "absolute." I assume, provisionally, that metaphor is absolute if it is autonomous, not dependent on likeness. Friedrich found autonomous metaphor in Mallarmé's *"Evanteil (de Madame Mallarmé)"* and in his untitled *"Surgi de la croupe et du bond."*

Here is a stanza from "Le Bateau ivre":

J'ai rêvé la nuit verte aux neiges éblouies,
Baiser montant aux yeux des mers avec lenteurs,
La circulation des sèves inouïes,
Et l'éveil jaune et bleu des phosphores chanteurs![11]

(In the green night I dreamed of blinding snows,
A slow kiss rising to the eyes of the ocean,
The circulation of bizarre sap,
Siren phosphorus, dawning blue and yellow.)[12]

That kiss, rising slowly to the eyes of the ocean, does not resemble any kiss ever given or received. It is whatever a reader deems it to be, exempt from rules of relation or likeness. If the phosphorus were singular rather than plural, it would mean the morning star: plural, they refer to any substances that give light without giving heat. They are "chanteurs" mainly because, rhyming with "lenteurs," they form an association in Rimbaud's mind. He could have rejected the association, but he let it stand, assenting to the charm of words so often said. "Ah! c'était si charmant, ces mots dit tant de fois!," as he wrote in his first poem, "Les Étrennes des orphelins." Not surprising: if you give up protecting "the rational" and "the logical" as Aristotle protected them; if you take your dreams as seriously as Freud did; and if you stop assuming that a metaphor must always be a nuance of resemblance, then you are well on the way toward eliminating the "adventitiousness of the empirical" and denying any privilege to the habitual or the natural. If you deliberately pitch your senses into derangement, one of the first casualties you must be prepared to put up with is your gratifying sense of resemblance—even your more daring power of divination by which, in the olden days, you intuited resemblance between otherwise unlike things. True, whatever then takes place in language, so long as we are under the sway of "absolute metaphor," "can never take place in any real world": there is merely— but why say "merely"?—resonance between one word and another, whether we call them tenor and vehicle or not; there is never an appeal to empirical axioms.[13]

Hans Blumenberg, taking Friedrich's evidence a step further, distinguishes between myth and "absolute metaphor":

> The difference between myth and "absolute metaphor" would here be a purely genetic one: myth bears the sanction of its primordial, unfathomable origin, its divine or inspirative ordination, whereas metaphor can present itself as a figment of the imagination, needing only to disclose a possibility of understanding in order for it to establish its credentials.[14]

"A possibility of understanding" is a generous criterion, especially if we think of modern painting and some modern music that withholds guidance—Braque, Picasso, Pollock, Malevich, Schoenberg, Webern, Berg. Surrealism has made a stronger flourish in painting than in literature because paint doesn't talk back, it doesn't rush, like a word, to the fleshpot of its old local reference. Modern music doesn't mind how long it stays dissonant. As Roberto Calasso has remarked, with Laforgue in mind, "a 'deft dissonance' becomes an attraction for the delicate sensibility, where once it would have been condemned out of hand in a rage of pedantry."[15]

Suppose you were reading, for the first time, the following poem, "Medallion," and were instructed to take it as the last poem of Pound's *Hugh Selwyn Mauberley (Life and Contacts)* (1920), or the last part of a second suite of poems called *Mauberley* (1920), or as a free-standing poem:

Luini in porcelain!
The grand piano
Utters a profane
Protest with her clear soprano.

The sleek head emerges
From the gold-yellow frock
As Anadyomene in the opening
Pages of Reinach.

Honey-red, closing the face-oval,
A basket-work of braids which seem as
    if they were

Spun in King Minos' hall
From metal, or intractable amber;

The face-oval beneath the glaze,
Bright in its suave bounding-line, as,
Beneath half-watt rays,
The eyes turn topaz.[16]

We read in *Mauberley* (1920) that Mauberley's "fundamental passion" was "This urge to convey the relation / of eye-lid and cheekbone / By verbal manifestations"; that is, "to present the series / of curious heads in medallion." The poem I've quoted is one of them. "A *collage* of optical analogies," Hugh Kenner called it, thereby releasing the first-time reader from the labor of deducing why one piece of language is placed beside another.[17] Collage is an affair of painting, where painters are not obliged to answer such questions: what you see is what you get. When the bits are assembled as the painter ordains, the work will be fine, he hopes. What he has put together will appear to have come together by a liaison of nature, the artist's genius, and good luck. But collage is harder in language, because each piece wants to run straight home to its reference. And analogies are not resemblances; they inhabit someone's mind for distant reasons, not necessarily likeness. The first-time reader may divine that the poem I've transcribed is Pound's attempt to present H. S. Mauberley as if he were a minor much-put-upon poet of the 1890s and a few years later trying to make a career for himself as a poet, fighting the odds. That is enough to be going on with.

The first stanza may be meaningful, but the meaning is not yet. We can only guess what force "Luini" is meant to exert. The first-time reader has a choice: she can read the poem as music, reciting the syllables like improvised notes, hoping, keeping her fingers crossed, that the notes will eventually make a charming experience, which they probably will. Or she can hold in her mind the bits of the lines she may happen to recognize. She may know that Anadyomene is another name for Venus, but she is unlikely to have read Salomon Reinach's *Apollo: An Illustrated Manual of the History of Art throughout the Ages,* an immensely successful book that ran to several editions in French and was translated into many languages including English, in which it appeared, translated by Florence Simmonds, in several editions of 1904, 1907, 1912, the last of which I happen to have in my hand. This is probably the one that Pound consulted.

If the first-time reader is confused, has no notion of Pound's theme, what he is talking about, or how a reader, full of goodwill, is supposed to proceed, Pound's riposte might be: well, go and find out. My particular interest centers on the management of the metaphors, if indeed they are metaphors, but it seems prudent to gather whatever information is available about the little poem. We can divine that a woman is playing a grand piano and that someone watching and listening is thinking that she might become the active figure in a medallion, perhaps one by Bernardo Luini (1475?–1532?), who is mentioned in *Apollo* with something close to contempt:

> Leonardo himself formed several pupils, or inspired several artists of talent, Beltraffio, Solario, Cesare da Sesto, Gaudenzio Ferrari, but also a large proportion of clumsy and mediocre imitators. The most popular of these disciples was and is Luini, who may be said to have translated the ideal of Leonardo into simple terms, a process he carried out not altogether

without vulgarity, for his elegance is superficial, his drawing
uncertain, and his power of invention limited. His most characteristic trait is a certain honeyed softness that delights the
multitude; but he rose to great heights in his frescoes in the
Church of Saronno, where he appears as the Filippino Lippi
of the Milanese School.[18]

Pound seems indifferent to Reinach's critical assessments, but
it's impossible otherwise to know the weight to attach to Luini.
The proposed relation between the pianist's sleek head and Reinach's rendition of Anadyomene isn't a likeness to be appreciated at
large in the world but an association in the listener's mind, to be
taken on trust: if it's in his mind for the moment, let it be. The
same with "a basket-work of braids," which seem to the listener
as if they were "Spun in King Midas's hall / From metal, or intractable amber." "Intractable" shows that he's looking at something or remembering it but not that he's requiring anyone else to
share his experience. The strong rhyme of the final "as" and "topaz" is not a visual analogy but a piece of acoustic good-luck, a
charm of circumstance.

"Like" does not appear in "Medallion." "As" does, three times.
"Like" is more predicative than "as": "as" rather than "like" testifies not only to a declared weakening of resemblance but to a
withdrawal, for this occasion, of the privilege of resembling. "As"
claims no more than that the entities in the case inhabit the speaker's mind at the same time and in some vague association. The first
"as" might have been "like" but isn't, for good reason. The second
introduces an indeed far-fetched but not-insisted-on correlation.
The third means: when the half-watt rays are turned on, the eyes
turn topaz.

Resemblance does not arise. Those items only are mentioned that happen to have come into Mauberley's mind, the occasion being his recollection of Renaissance art, casual bits of it. "Medallion" is a "pure poem" appropriate to the nineties. Nothing that comes into the poem is alien to its general tone: its scholarly references are easily assimilated, no reader is obliged to go to a big library and dig out a copy of Reinach.

Closer to home than "Le Bateux ivre," is—as a figment of the imagination, I would suggest, capable of being understood, if not easily perceptible—the first stanza of Keats's "Ode on a Grecian Urn." This is an instance of "absolute metaphor" or "autonomous metaphor" as I would prefer to call it: metaphor that bears no resemblance—no semblance—to what it ostensibly refers to or issues from. On the page, we have just the title, then these apostrophes to the urn and, in the later lines of the stanza, the figures Keats sees or imagines on it:

> Thou still unravish'd bride of quietness,
>   Thou foster-child of silence and slow time,
> Sylvan historian, who canst thus express
>   A flowery tale more sweetly than our rhyme:
> What leaf-fring'd legend haunts about thy shape
>   Of deities or mortals, or of both,
>   In Tempe or the dales of Arcady?
> What men or gods are these? What maidens loath?
> What mad pursuit? What struggle to escape?
>   What pipes and timbrels? What wild
>   ecstasy?[19]

The first line gives a textual choice. When the poem was first published, in *Annals of the Fine Arts* 15 (January, 1820) under the heading, "On a Grecian Urn," it had a comma after "still." That turned "still" into an adjective qualifying "bride." It also had the effect of making the past participle "unravished" do the work of an adjective. In the 1920 volume the comma is removed, making "still" an adverb modifying "unravished" and restoring "unravished" to its status as past participle, but the whole line is then in danger of exclaiming: are you *still* an unravished bride? The bridegroom Quietness would be unlikely ever to ravish his bride.

The first four lines address the pot. A funerary urn, it is feminine, an erotic receptacle, mainly because any receptacle is erotic. A virgin bride, still "unravished." What would it mean to ravish an urn? To smash it in bits? Miriam Allott thinks that the lines are legible because "the urn is intact—a term applicable to pottery and virgins—which implies its lasting union with quiet." Hard to credit, since no word like "intact" appears, and a "lasting union with quiet" is what we are told has not been effected, nor ever will be. Keats, Mrs. Allott goes on, "telescopes the notions of an 'unravished bride of time' and 'bride of quietness' at the risk of suggesting that quiet itself may be a ravisher." The risk is a certainty. The pristine or virginal quality of the urn, she maintains, is linked below with the virgins on its frieze. Further: "The artist who made the urn died long ago, leaving it to be fostered by time and silence. [Line 2] expresses paradoxically the perennial youthfulness of the urn together with its antique serenity."[20] It is strange that no telescoping of lines or other changing of Keats's words is suggested for the later lines of the stanza. These lines do not convey "the pristine or virginal quality of the urn"; on the contrary, they set up conditions of sexual riot or orgy, culminating in "What wild ecstasy?" The lines posit two levels of motivation—"What men or gods are these?"—but the sexual riot is so extreme that it can with equal convincingness be ascribed to both kinds—"Of

deities or mortals, or of both."[21] The riot is held back only because the figures on the urn are, of necessity, frozen in their little
spaces.

Taking this slowly: in the two first lines the poet is looking at
the urn. The urn is the tenor of the metaphor; everything else is the
vehicle. The urn is complete in itself, entirely what it is, in all its
qualities. Silence is its chief quality; it does not say anything. Sur-
rounded on all sides by noise, it has the grace to keep to itself. But
there are silences and silences. George Steiner has interpreted
"unravished bride of quietness" as a philosophic ideal: with Mallarmé's *Igitur* and his blank spaces in view, Steiner construes the
silence of the urn as the principle of truth, set against the lies of
common blather, "politically prostituted language." He refers to
the "monstrous amplification of the trivial," set against "the decencies, the cognitive and moral cleanliness of silence." Silence surrounds the blather, and rebukes it. Whether or not it is as eloquent
and truthful as Steiner thinks it is, there is no evidence: "Between
suspect speech acts, blank spaces—Mallarmé's famous *les blancs*—
are custodians or heralds of silence. Which is in turn the poetry
of the unspoken."[22] But Keats's states of being are invariably on
tiptoe—as G. Wilson Knight noted—they are just about to do
something they never do or say something they never say. In the
third line the urn begins to have something to report ("Sylvan
historian") and for the rest of the stanza it turns the figures on the
side of it into suspended ecstasy. Thereafter, the poem becomes a
meditation on the tension between the urn, the work of art as an
eternal thing, and the pathetic contingency of mere life.

Helen Vendler has noted that "in other odes, and at the beginning of this ode, Keats is often a passive subject, content to be
worked upon by his imaginings":

"Bride of quietness" is a far more complex formulation than "Dryad of the trees" or "amorous glow-worm of the sky"; and yet "bride of quietness," "foster-child of silence," and "sylvan historian" are still epithets of wonder and empathy and pathos, rather than epithets engendered by a critical mind.[23]

Wonder, empathy, and pathos may indeed be somewhere in the contexture of the words, but even if they are, they do not testify to any resemblance, they are place holders for the resemblance they transcend. It is possible—just barely possible—that in these first lines Keats is not looking at the urn but at one of the figures on it. Unlikely, since we are to assume that he sees the urn at a distance before moving up close to it. The second half of the stanza evades the issue of resemblance by asking several rhetorical questions designed to animate the figures on the urn into an erotic history, only to be frozen in its exclamations.

Anyone might ask: what can there be but resemblance, if these words are to be justified? The first answer that occurs to me is an appeal to the plenitude of the poet's mind: unravishment, bride, quietness, silence, and slow time are linkages of feeling in Keats's mind, which he associates with the integrity of the urn as a sculpted object that for the moment keeps its counsel. But these associations are only in the poet's mind, they have that sole authority and it is enough, they are provoked by the urn in some occult way without resembling it. Vendler's phrasing is apposite only in part: "a passive subject, content to be worked upon by his imaginings." But then Keats works upon these imaginings sufficiently by not rejecting them: he accepts them as if they were gifts of God or the gods, which they may well be. If they are, how could he deny them? "Sylvan historian": at this late stage in its life, the pot is not going to tell lies. John Jones is so determined to find the apostrophes reasonable that he thinks the urn is Adam's Eve, by appeal to Keats's letter of November 22, 1817, to Benjamin Bailey: "The Imagination may be compared to Adam's dream . . . he awoke and found it truth." Jones speaks of the first four words—"Thou still unravish'd bride"—as "tugging sharply at the temporal continuum along which they are strung." I see the continuum, but I don't feel the tug. Jones seems to mean that in this ode Keats is trying to write an urn, a sculpture, and therefore a simultaneous, spatial entity, even though to do so he must use words, a temporal medium:

> Obviously—I dare say obviously—he is not thinking about the interval between a marriage's celebration and its consummation; his words are after the ripe and spatial solution—there she was—of Adam's dream; they are intended to say what the urn is; and we, reading, are meant to rub our eyes and find "it truth."[24]

"Obviously—I dare say obviously": Keats must have some very arcane and therefore compelling reason for "unravish'd" if it doesn't mean what it appears to mean. Jones thinks his reason is that "the time-words which litter the *Grecian Urn* only take on life and sense through a process of derivation from space." He doesn't say what the derivation of "unravish'd" from space might be, unless he only means—with Miriam Allott—that the urn is still intact, unbroken—a point hardly worth making with the Elgin marbles in everyone's eyes. In any case, none of these strivings brings the apostrophes any closer to resemblance. We are left with the only remaining authority, our taking it for granted that these associations were in Keats's mind and that he was content to be worked upon by them. How they came to be in his mind is a question that may not have a persuasive answer.

But there is another possibility: that we retain the first four lines within the idiom of metaphor, and construe the three vehicles as instances of catachresis, the "figure of abuse" in histories of rhetoric, normally considered a vice of style but one that Puttenham allowed if the need of it were great. It is usually found where the resources of more decorous metaphors are not thought to be enough, and the poet sweeps aside any expected objection to its excess—Milton's "blind mouths," for instance. Or irreverent objections to the Litany of the Blessed Virgin. Or the conceits in metaphysical poems, toward which there can be no reasonable objection, even where Crashaw is the poet in question. Keats's urn bears no resemblance to a bride, a foster child, or a historian. It is fair to call these figures metaphors only if we call them, more accurately, catachreses, allowing them to be scandalous to resemblance, however tight or loose we draw our conception of resemblance.

The abuse began with the irruption of "unravished" into the middle of the first line, where it had no business to be: it has nothing to do with the context of the first four lines. It would be fine if it found a place anywhere from lines five to ten, where it belongs. This is what those lines are about: unravishment, ravishment forestalled, held forever in the violent sexual suspense of the lines. In the first line, Keats was running ahead of himself, flying in the face of an erotic presumption.

I have referred to "association" in relation to the passages I've quoted from Rimbaud and Keats: it seems a harmless enough word, but it has had a contentious presence in psychology. From the beginning of the eighteenth century to the later years of the nineteenth, the force of association in the construction of ideas was either accepted or rejected; at least the argument had to be faced, if only to be refuted. Everyone wanted to believe that human reason was an independent power, God-given or not, fully capable of judging one's experience, but this belief was hard to maintain in light of some evidence to the contrary. In 1700 John Locke added a chapter, "Of the Association of Ideas," to his *Essay Concerning Human Understanding,* disturbed as he was by the tendency of certain ideas to run together for no sufficient reason:

> Some of our *Ideas* have a natural Correspondence and Connexion one with another: It is the Office and Excellency of our Reason to trace these, and hold them together in that Union and Correspondence which is founded in their peculiar Beings. Besides this there is another Connexion of *Ideas* wholly owing to Chance or Custom; *Ideas* that in themselves are not at all of kin, come to be so united in some Mens Minds, that 'tis very hard to separate them, they always keep in company, and the one no sooner at any time comes into the Understanding but its Associate appears with it; and if there are more than two which are thus united, the whole gang always inseparable shew themselves together.[25]

The leap from "company" to "gang" shows that Locke too is afflicted by the association of images: he is exerting critical pressure on them, trying to prize them loose and send each of them running away.

David Hume, in his *Inquiry Concerning Human Understanding* (1748), gave a copious account of the three principles upon which ideas rush into association: resemblance, contiguity in time or place, and cause and effect. David Hartley argued in *Observations on Man* (1749) that knowledge is the result of repeated juxtapositions of corpuscular vibrations, an explanation that exposed the possibility that these forms of knowledge could be enforced: brainwashing is the modern name of this process. Joseph Priestley's *Hartley's Theory of the Human Mind* (1775) presented the case in neurophysiology and psychology for cognitive acts made possible by the "joint impression" of sensations. Associationist psychology in the nineteenth century worked on the consequences of these notions. In the *Enquiry Concerning Political Justice (1793)* Godwin brought forward even worse news: that every idea, however complex, offers itself to the mind under the axiom of unity. The mind's prejudice in favor of unity made thinking virtually impossible. By 1805 the mischief of the association of ideas—or of images, since ideas are only congealed images—was so rampant that Hazlitt had to attack Hartley's version of it directly in the hope of claiming autonomous force for volition, mind, and imagination. In the *Essay on the Principles of Human Action* he insisted that volition could not be explained "from mere association."[26] Coleridge was for many years persuaded by Hartley on association, but in the end—in two chapters of *Biographia Literaria*—he rejected his arguments. Hartley, he said, differed from Aristotle's *De Anima* "only to err." His system would issue in "the despotism of the outward senses," and would reduce the will "and with the will all acts of thought and attention" to being "parts and products of this blind mechanism, instead of being distinct powers, whose function it is to controul, determine, and modify the phantasmal chaos of association."[27] All might still be well if you could, as C. S. Peirce offered to do in "Some Consequences of Four Incapacities"

(1868), present the association of ideas as in fact an association of judgments amounting to inference:

> The association of ideas is said to proceed according to three principles—those of resemblance, of contiguity, and of causality. But it would be equally true to say that signs denote what they do on the three principles of resemblance, contiguity, and causality. There can be no question that anything is a sign of whatever is associated with it by resemblance, by contiguity, or by causality: nor can there be any doubt that any sign recalls the thing signified. So, then, the association of ideas consists in this, that a judgment occasions another judgment, of which it is the sign. Now this is nothing less nor more than inference.[28]

This ingenious attempt to turn an embarrassment into a respectable form of judgment to be understood by a theory of semiotics did not end the dispute. For one thing, the images and ideas that come together as one of Locke's "gangs" often, as in dreams and fantasies, bear no resemblance to one another. They are a mob, an irregular bunch of associates, come from God knows where. There were further interrogations by William James and F. H. Bradley. But perhaps the most severe attack on the association of ideas was Remy de Gourmont's in an essay of 1899 in which he urged the "dissociation" of those ideas; that is, that wherever an idea presents itself—usually as a commonplace, a truism, or what we call an ideology (according to which one enforces a mere axiom of culture as if it had the privilege of a law of nature)—we should deal with it analytically, as a chemist would take a compound and break it down to its elements. The aim of this activity was to ensure that one's intelligence would be kept supple and would "lead toward that state of disdainful nobility toward which it should aspire."[29] Yeats worried about "a new naturalism that leaves man helpless before the contents of his own mind," and he thought that Pound's *Cantos* (so far as he had read them) and Joyce's "Anna Livia Plurabelle" (assuming he read it) were "works of an heroic sincerity, the man, his active faculties in suspense, one finger beating time to a bell sounding and echoing in the depths of his own mind."[30]

I am not claiming that Rimbaud and Keats were troubled by the association of ideas; on the contrary. Indeed, to write the stanzas I have quoted, they would have had to relax the criteria under which they kept their "active faculties" at full stretch. Specifically, they would have had to release themselves from the law of resemblance and lend themselves, at least for the moment, to the more concessive axiom of association. If the privilege of comparison were to be retained, it would have to be construed as André Breton recommended in a passage from *Les vases communicants* that Richards quoted only to deplore: "To compare two objects, as remote from one another in character as possible, or by any other method put them together in a sudden and striking fashion, this remains the highest task to which poetry can aspire."[31] Richards found this essay in surrealism scandalous. He insisted that "the mind will always try to find connections and will be guided in its search by the rest of the utterance and its occasion."[32]

But Richards's appeal to the decorum implied by context is not convincing. He seems to be saying, "Yes, put things together in a metaphor that are quite far apart but not disgracefully far apart." I think the first line of Keats's "Ode" invokes things disgracefully far apart. But my talk of relaxation isn't appropriate. To write the first lines of "Ode on a Grecian Urn," Keats had to strike out on his own, as the phrase "unravish'd bride" makes clear. It takes muscle to place things in apposition rather than to find them resembling. Roland Barthes describes a "good" metaphor as "one where language labors, struggles, isn't inert." "Basically, one would have to analyze the *force* that, within an image, makes it more or less resistant to stereotyping."[33]

A recent poem by Frederick Seidel may be a good case in point. It is called, "Moto Poeta" and subtitled, "In Memory of Stephen A. Aaron (1936–2012)." Aaron was one of Seidel's friends at Harvard, "the most gifted man in Harvard theater / In thirty years." The first seven stanzas of Seidel's nine are memorial tributes, until the eighth exclaims:

Steve,

> You're a blue forest of oceans, seagulls flying their cries.
> I come from an unimaginably different plan.
> I've traveled to you because my technology can.

And then to certify that technology, the poem ends:

> I ride the cosmos on my poetry Ducati, Big Bang engine,
>   einsteinium forks.
> Let me tell you about the extraterrestrial Beijings and New
>   Yorks.
> You are dear planet Earth, where my light-beam spaceship
>   will land.
> I'll land, after light-years of hovering, and take your hand.[34]

No resemblance there. "You're a blue forest of oceans, seagulls flying their cries" because Seidel lets rip, "technology" doing the work traditionally done by the poetic imagination. "Unimaginably" is a joke, since the different plan has itself to be imagined.

The "poetry Ducati" is Seidel's name for his favorite images, made to measure for him in Italy's premier motor-cycle shop. He requires them to resist the stereotyping that might otherwise be enforced by Romantic odes, Shelleyan skylarks, anybody's seagulls. The resistance is strong enough to turn "flying" into a transitive verb. "Blue" is the imagination's color, as in Stevens, as if to show that Seidel need not dismiss the tradition he appears to transcend. Riding the cosmos—Big Bang engine, einsteinium forks—is Seidel's answer to Shelley's "Ode to the West Wind," exempt from Shelley's needs. The spaceship lands because it has been everywhere, done everything. Luckily, it has some dear one to come home to on planet Earth.

"It Ensures That Nothing Goes without a Name"

The most fascinating property of language is its
capacity to make metaphors. But what an under-
statement! For metaphor is not a mere extra trick of
language, as it is so often slighted in the old school-
books on composition; it is the very constitutive
ground of language.

—Julian Jaynes

Poetry is finer than prose because it gives us more
concrete truth in the same compass of words.
Metaphor, its chief device, is at once the substance of
nature and of language. Poetry only does consciously
what the primitive races did unconsciously. The
chief work of literary men in dealing with language,
and of poets especially, lies in feeling back along the
ancient lines of advance. He must do this so that he
may keep his words enriched by all their subtle
undertones of meaning. The original metaphors
stand as a kind of luminous background, giving color
and vitality, forcing them closer to the concreteness
of natural processes. Shakespeare everywhere teems
with examples.

—Ernest Fenollosa

> The poet, in dealing with his own time, must also
> see to it that language does not petrify on his hands.
> He must prepare for new advances along the lines of
> true metaphor, that is interpretative metaphor, or
> image, as diametrically opposed to untrue, or
> ornamental, metaphor.
>
> —Ezra Pound, commenting on Fenollosa above

*t*he second chapter of *Genesis* reports that God brought "every beast of the field, and every fowl of the air" to Adam "to see what he would call them." "Whatsoever Adam called every living creature, that was the name thereof." Presumably the name gave official reference to each thing, according to its kind. Pointing to a particular thing, Adam declared it to be, I assume, an animal and, as a particular instance among animals, a cow. Figures of speech and figures of thought were not required; the name covered everything, literally, that needed to be said. Anything in the world could be named without equivocation. So, according to the eleventh chapter of *Genesis,* "the whole earth was of one language, and of one speech." But that chapter also reports that the people who lived in the land of Shinar decided to build a city and a tower "whose top *may reach* unto heaven." The Lord came down to see what was going on, though He knew in advance the vanity he would find:

> And the Lord said, Behold, the people *is* one, and they have
> all one language; and this they begin to do: and now nothing
> will be restrained from them, which they have imagined to
> do. Go to, let us go down, and there confound their language,

that they may not understand one another's speech. So the
Lord scattered them abroad from thence upon the face of all
the earth.

He also "did there confound the language of all the earth." Instead of one universal language, there would be thousands of them.
Instead of one comprehensive name for each thing, we have a ru-
dimentary system of nomenclature eked out by a multitude of
figures. "But I gotta use words when I talk to you," T. S. Eliot's
Sweeney says, but the words don't seem to be adequate. Some
people—few indeed, though they include Leibniz and Luther—
think that beneath the multiplicity of idiolects there may still be
discerned the ur-language of names that Adam prescribed.[1] Many
people, including Locke, ridicule the hope, and regard such com-
parative linguistics as an empty, mystical pursuit. Speakers of different languages utter different sounds when they see a cow. The
relation between thing and word in any of the multitudinous
languages is entirely conventional; it has no relation to nature.
There is nothing natural in the origin of words: the propinquity
of signifier and signified is entirely arbitrary.

The Adamic theory of the origin of language gives privilege to
the act of naming, and establishes the name as the *tenor* of the thing.
Aristotle agrees, and regards the figures as deviations, often justified, from a proper norm that is found in common usage, the
speech of a people. According to the eleventh book of *Genesis,*
God seems to have thought he had punished the people of Shinar
sufficiently by scattering them and confounding their language.
He didn't interfere with the new idiolects or set any limits to their
profusion. Perhaps He had lost interest. In any event, metaphor was
one of those profusions, and it soon established itself as chief

among them. Resemblance between one thing and another must have been thought an aspect of particular salience. I concede that, for the most part, the relation between tenor and vehicle that constitutes a metaphor is mostly a function of resemblance, but not always.

I hope it will turn out that Vico was right in at least one of his conjectures about the origin of language:

> From all this it appears to have been demonstrated that, by a necessity of human nature, poetic style arose before prose style; just as, by the same necessity, the fables, or imaginative universals, arose before the rational or philosophic universals which were formed through the medium of prose speech. For after the poets had formed poetic speech by associating particular ideas, as we have fully shown, the peoples went on to form prose speech by contracting into a single word, as into a genus, the parts which poetic speech had associated. Take for example the poetic phrase, "the blood boils in my heart," based on a property natural, eternal and common to all mankind. They took the blood, the boiling and the heart, and made of them a single word, as it were a genus, called in Greek *stomachos,* in Latin *ira* and in Italian *collera.*[2]

Condillac too acknowledged in his *Essai sur l'origine des connaissances humaines* (1746) that "it is to the poets that we owe the first and perhaps also the greatest obligations."[3] Rousseau gave the idea further currency in his *Essai sur l'origine des langues* (completed probably about 1763, published in 1781) when he said that "the language of the first men is represented to us as the tongues of geometers, but we see that they were the tongues of poets. We did not begin by reasoning but by feeling . . . The first languages were tuneful and passionate before being simple and methodical."

The third chapter of Rousseau's *Essai* begins:

> As the first motives that made man speak were the passions, his first expressions were Tropes. Figurative language was the first to arise, proper meaning was found last. Things were not called by their true name until they were seen in their genuine form. At first, only poetry was spoken. Only long afterwards did anyone take it into his head to reason.[4]

The first language had to be figurative because it was implicated in feelings, desires, fears, and illusions; it was not occupied in making straightforward statements or in pointing to objects. In time, the felt need to make accurate statements led to the development of prose, curbing the excesses of poetry; the new prose made life relatively easy for writers of logic, philosophy and, eventually, science. Gradually, prose displaced verse, becoming the norm, and verse was regarded as an indulgence, an occasional flourish, metaphor a gesture, a fling of freedom from the constraints of naming and demonstration. Aristotle, again, was the arbiter of such disciplines.

Vico's boldest intervention in the understanding of rhetoric was his assertion, debonair indeed, that all the tropes are reducible to four moments in *elocutio:* metaphor, metonymy, synecdoche, and irony, listed in that order for no clear reason. Of course he knew many other figures, but he thought they could be reduced to one or another of these four. He was wrong, but he was resolute in claiming that his chosen four were the key instruments. He didn't offer any evidence for his choice of this quartet, but it has become almost mandatory. Kenneth Burke took it up in *Permanence and Change* and *A Grammar of Motives,* and Hayden White in *Metahistory* and *Tropics of Discourse.* I think the leap to metaphor as the first term is questionable, and that a more prosaic order of items may be better. Burke thought that the order doesn't matter. "The four tropes shade into one another"; "Give a man but one of them, tell him to exploit its possibilities, and if he is thorough in doing so, he will come upon the other three."[5] He may, but I don't think any man, however resourceful, could come upon all the other figures—I haven't counted them—that handbooks of rhetoric include. In any case, Vico should not be scolded for ignoring the figures that modern readers, myself included, have chosen not to memorize; we look them up when we need to. I propose a different order.

Simile

One must start somewhere. I find two suggestive possibilities. In *Phenomenology of Spirit* Hegel posits "Die sinnliche Gewissheit" or "sense-certainty," only to refute it on second thought, but it persists as an attractive notion, and we turn it to the best light we have. It seems to denote the senses in their undifferentiating openness to the world, prior to perception and understanding. The senses are open to any impression that happens to impinge, apparently without exercising preference. Hegel says:

> The knowledge or knowing which is at the start or is immediately our object cannot be anything else but immediate knowledge itself, a knowledge of the immediate or of what simply *is.* Our approach to the object must also be *immediate* or *receptive;* we must alter nothing in the object as it presents itself. In *appre-*hending it, we must refrain from trying to *com*prehend it.[6]

Hegel gives sense certainty its due:

> Because of its concrete content, sense-certainty immediately
> appears as the *richest* kind of knowledge, indeed a knowledge
> of infinite wealth for which no bounds can be found, either
> when we *reach out* into space and time in which it is dispersed,
> or when we take a bit of this wealth, and by division *enter into*
> it. Moreover, sense-certainty appears to be the *truest* knowl-
> edge; for it has not as yet omitted anything from the object,
> but has the object before it in its perfect entirety.

But then the second thought enforced itself on him:

> In the event, this very *certainty* proves itself to be the most
> abstract and poorest *truth*. All that it says about what it knows
> is just that it *is;* and its truth contains nothing but the sheer
> *being* of the thing [*Sache*].[7]

This seems to admit an equivocation: are we discussing what the
faculty of sense certainty says about itself or what it enjoys in silence? Hegel doesn't raise this question. Is it really damaging to
claim that the only thing sense can report about what it knows is
just that it *is?* In some philosophies that might amount to a trium-
phant conclusion.

I fancy that the sensory capacity, according to Hegel, waking
up and rubbing the sleep from her eyes, looks about and stares,
appalled maybe, at the plethora of impressions demanding her
attention—and the day has only just begun. How to proceed
with this saturation? She notes that some impressions are a bit like
some other ones, and she starts her busy day on that little note. It
doesn't come to much, this being like that and another being like
something else. But it's a start, and a later stage of cognition will

dignify it with the word *similitudo,* exercising a privilege in favor of Latin. In Greek and Latin, to bring forward a resemblance between one thing and another is normally done to further a proof in a speech. If in a Latin sentence you say *ut . . . sic,* you imply that you have the whole force of natural law—or at least of universal custom—on your side. This figure of comparison starts out modestly and stays the course. "The simile is a formal, leisurely figure, which sets side by side with equal prominence the two objects compared."[8] Recall the philosopher Austin's affection for the word "like," how it helps us to get by when we can't say precisely what we mean:

> If we think of words as being shot like arrows at the world, the function of these adjuster-words [like *like*] is to free us from the disability of being able to shoot only straight ahead. . . . The word "like" equips us *generally* to handle the unforeseen, in a way in which new words invented *ad hoc* don't, and can't.[9]

Similitudines hold level ground, even when all around them are orating. When Cassius says to Brutus, of Julius Caesar, "Why, man, he doth bestride the narrow world / Like a Colossus," the narrow word *like* keeps the discourse temperate, and allows Brutus to make his answer cooler still: "What you would work me to, I have some aim" (Shakespeare, *Julius Caesar,* I.ii.142). In Emily Dickinson's poem the double "as" is just as quieting as "like." "As imperceptibly as Grief / The Summer lapsed away" (J.1540), but a reader might interrupt her to say, "Excuse me, my grief is just as acute tonight as it ever was, after many a summer." Chapter 12 of *Ulysses* ends:

> And there came a voice out of heaven, calling: *Elijah! Elijah!*
> And He answered with a main cry: *Abba! Adonai!* And they

> beheld Him even Him, ben Bloom Elijah, amid clouds of
> angels ascend to the glory of the brightness at an angle of
> forty-five degrees over Donohoe's in Little Green street like a
> shot off a shovel.[10]

The cooling-off begins with the redundant precision of "at an angle of forty-five degrees," continues with Donohoe's in Little Green street, and imposes itself for good—despite the momentary grandeur of the alliteration—with the shot off a shovel. The only shots off shovels to be witnessed by Dubliners in 1904 being those of grave diggers in Glasnevin and workers employed to remove the droppings of horses and cows from the streets of the city, shots none of them especially energetic.

The other possibility comes to me from Ernst Cassirer. In the second volume of *The Philosophy of Symbolic Forms* he posits a condition prior to the Hegelian one in which the senses engage with objects or impressions as things-that-add-up-to-contents. What the senses meet first, according to Cassirer, is felt as force, not as impressions. Cassirer calls the senses in that state mythic consciousness, which meets not impressions that testify to objects but gods that don't testify at all. Derrida said that "*form* fascinates when one no longer has the force to understand force from within itself."[11] We deal with objects—or apparent objects—more easily than with force, which is likely to appear uncanny. The point of departure for all science, Cassirer says, "the immediacy from which it starts, lies not so much in the sensory sphere as in the sphere of mythical intuition."[12] At one point he pushes Hegel aside to make a space for mythical thought:

> To be sure, epistemological inquiries often find the begin-
> ning of all knowledge in a state of pure immediacy in which

impressions are received and experienced in their simple sensory properties—without any formation or intellectual elaboration of any sort. In this state, supposedly, all contents are still situated on one plane; they are still endowed with a single undifferentiated character of simple material existence. But it is too readily forgotten that the purely "naïve" stage of the empirical consciousness here presupposed is itself no fact but a theoretical construction, that it is fundamentally nothing other than a limiting concept created by epistemological reflection.[13]

The point is well taken, but it doesn't erase *similitudines,* it merely postpones them. Instead of Hegel's "sense-certainty," Cassirer adumbrates a progressive *analysis* of the elements of experience, "a critical operation of the intellect in which the 'accidental' is progressively differentiated from the 'essential,' the variable from the constant."[14] Cassirer was too much a man of the Enlightenment to want to postpone indefinitely the march of science: he mainly wanted to give myth a decent burial before welcoming Hegel's progress toward the possession of all the differentiations and distinctions that lead to full empirical science.

Among these—subjective and objective, inner and outer, like and unlike—the distinction between like and unlike is the one that moves most directly into the resources of rhetoric. Simile says that this is like that, in the one respect that strikes me—as in Dante's *Inferno* when the pilgrims meet "a troop of souls that were coming alongside the bank, and each looked at us as men look at one another under a new moon at dusk; and they knit their brows at us as the old tailor does at the eye of his needle"—"come 'l vecchio sartor fa ne la cruna."[15] For the moment, no other attribute of tailors is invoked. The things which the mind peruses at this early point are not given to it without encumbrance; they are received, subject to the theoretical forces that Cassirer has described. But these forces cannot deflect the mind from pursuing likenesses and unlikenesses among the impressions it receives. Simile denotes not just the likeness of one impression and another but the desire of the mind to find such likeness. Seeing is believing, but it is also the fulfillment of the desire to believe. Or sometimes the desire to extend the simile to a further point along its line, as if to give it more experience than that of saying that *this* is like *that*. Shelley's "To the Moon" cherishes such a motive:

> Art thou pale for weariness
> Of climbing heaven, and gazing on the earth,
> Wandering companionless
> Among the stars that have a different birth,—
> And ever-changing, like a joyless eye
> That finds no object worth its constancy?[16]

Here the simile has no difficulty in accommodating the plenitude of personification, "joyless" doing most of the work.

Metonymy

Hard to distinguish, in a poor light, from synecdoche. Metonymy is a figure by which the part is taken to be the whole: "boots on the ground" meaning soldiers on the battle scene. It is interpreted in either of two moods: loose or strict. Loose, as in my fanciful notion of mind in the Hegelian scene of sense-certainty, now fully awake and perhaps grown tired of looking around for likenesses, who may be intrigued by things she sees together. This interest, later to be given a professional tone and called "the figure of contiguity," is an impulse to examine what goes with what—irrespective of likeness—and why they are together. She may even wonder whether these things have come together by nature or have been put there by hands similar to her own, like the peremptory edges in a Cubist painting. It would make a difference. If by nature or the appearance of having come together as if by nature, the collocation would gain that large prestige. If the items have been put together by human hands, the prestige accorded would generally be much smaller. For the moment, we may compare metonymy with the association of images or ideas, and wonder under either terminology what goes with what, and why.

Roman Jakobson has reduced Vico's four to two, metaphor and metonymy, and is loose with metonymy. He accepts as a metonymy nearly any two things found keeping company, even though he is often dismayed by the consequences of their intimacy. In two essays, "On Realism in Art" and "Two Aspects of Language and Two Types of Aphasic Disturbances," he refers to Tolstoy's narrative of the suicide of Anna Karenina. He takes this episode to illustrate—in his italics—*"the condensation of the narrative by means of images based on contiguity, that is, avoidance of the normal designative term in favor of metonymy or synecdoche"*: "Let us take a crude example from Russian literature, that of the suicides of Poor Liza and Anna Karenina. Describing Anna's suicide, Tolstoy primarily writes about her handbag. Such an unessential detail would have made no sense to Karamzin. . . ."[17] Not quite true. Tolstoy refers twice, in this long paragraph, to Anna's "little red bag," each time with good point. Anna intends throwing herself among the carriages of the first train:

> She wanted to fall under the first carriage, the midpoint of which had drawn even with her. But the red bag, which she

started taking off her arm, delayed her and it was too late: the midpoint went by. She had to wait for the next carriage. A feeling seized her, similar to what she experienced when preparing to go into the water for a swim, and she crossed herself. The habitual gesture of making the sign of the cross called up in her soul a whole series of memories from childhood and girlhood, and suddenly the darkness that covered everything for her broke and life rose up before her momentarily with all its bright past joys. Yet she did not take her eyes from the wheels of the approaching second carriage. And just at the moment when the midpoint between the two wheels came even with her, she threw the red bag aside and, drawing her head down between her shoulders, fell on her hands under the carriage, and with a light movement, as if preparing to get up again at once, sank to her knees.[18]

It is to be expected that a woman in a realist novel will carry a little red bag, even to the railway station where she intends to take her life, and that taking the bag off her arm will impede her decision to throw herself in front of the middle carriage of the first train; and that flinging the bag away would be her last act before throwing herself among the carriages of the second. Anna's body and the bag make a metonymy, loosely construed: one thing, then another noticed beside it. Not at all crude, as Jakobson thought; it is just as convincing as another metonymy: her crossing herself and recalling the joys of her childhood and youth.

Besides, it fulfills the requirements of metonymy, strictly defined, as Quintilian defines it: "There is no great gap between Synecdoche and Metonymy, which is the substitution of one name for another (the force of which is to put the reason for which something is said in place of that which is said [cuius vis est pro eo quod dicitur causam propter quam dicitur ponere])" (8.6.23). The point of the parenthetical words is to indicate that the words brought together to make a metonymy should be words from different levels of reference. If—these are Quintilian's examples—you call corn Ceres, or wine Bacchus, you observe this requirement. Du Marsais gives many other examples including "a beautiful Rembrandt" for one of the master's paintings. He also extends the categories that make metonymies: cause for effect, effect for cause, container for the thing contained, place for the thing associated with it, sign for the thing signified, abstract word for the concrete, parts of the body as sites of passion—"du coeur" for "du courage," a man's name for his house—this one, transcribed from Quintilian, Aeneid (2.311–312), has "iam proximus ardet Ucalegon," meaning that Ucalegon's house next door is on fire.[19] When Cicero wants to say that the civil, peaceful virtues are preferable to the military ones, he uses a metonymy: "cedant arma togae."

The clearest type of metonymy common to poets and orators "is that by which we indicate cause by effect," as in Aeneid, 6.275, "pallentesque habitant Morbi tristisque Senectus" (there pale diseases dwell and sad old age.) This could also be considered a personification, where "an animal or an inanimate object is represented as having human attributes or addressed as if it were human."[20] But it lends itself to loose treatment, since it is doubtful that the two nouns can be said to be on different levels. Brian Vickers has rebuked Jakobson for taking the loose way:

> In rhetoric . . . metonymy involves the substitution of a
> "related" term . . . according to fixed transitions or tropings
> within a category on different levels, such as putting the

container for the thing contained, or the sign for the thing signified. In Jakobson's examples there is no such movement across the levels within a category. . . .[21]

The crucial thing, according to Fontanier in his notes to du Marsais, is that the two parties to the metonymy be kept separate—"mais tel cependant que les deux objets existent séparément l'un de l'autre, et ne sont point censés ne former ensemble qu'un seul et même tout"—there must be no seepage into metaphor, no fusion or interaction of the elements.[22] Thus Kenneth Burke is on firm traditional ground in saying that the basic "strategy" in metonymy is "to convey some incorporeal or intangible state in terms of the corporeal or tangible." As to speak of "the heart" rather than "the emotions."[23]

But it is hard to maintain a difference between metonymy and synecdoche, or to prevent metonymy from slipping into metaphor. We are not on firm ground. Gérard Genette has argued that in Proust metaphor finds "son appui et sa motivation dans une métonymie." Proust rarely makes his metaphors by transferring a word from its proper place to another—which is metaphor according to classical rhetoric. The constituents of his metaphors are normally "plus objectif et plus sûr"—that is, "les choses voisines et les mots liés." In Proust, involuntary memory does the work of metaphor: metaphor is in art what reminiscence is in life, "rapprochement de deux sensations par le 'miracle d'une analogie.'" Genette notes that this *rapprochement* is "pure de toute métonymie," not metaphor.[24] Involuntary memory brings two distant sensations together, but it is their felt equivalence that counts; one of them does not play vehicle to the other's tenor.

Synecdoche

Quintilian is again our best guide. He said, following Cicero, that "metaphor ought either to occupy a vacant space or, if it replaces something else, to be more effective than the word it banishes." Then:

> I can say this almost more forcefully of Synecdoche. While metaphor is designed generally to affect the emotions, put a clear mark on things, and place them before our eyes, Synecdoche has the power to vary the discourse, enabling the hearer to understand many things from one, the whole from the part, the genus from the species, the consequences from the antecedents, and vice versa. Poets have more scope for it than orators (8.6.20).

Like Cicero, Quintilian protects orators from interference by poets. Poets, concerned only with pleasure, can say many things that would be offensive in a speech in court: "It may be all right to say 'blade' for 'sword' or 'roof' for 'house' in prose, but not 'stern' for 'ship' or 'fir' for 'wooden tablets'; again, 'steel' will do for 'sword,' but not 'quadruped' for horse." (At this point the Loeb editor intervenes to remark that Latin *quadrupes* is poetical, quite unlike English "quadruped.") In prose, according to Quintilian:

> It is liberty of number which will be most useful. Livy often says "The Roman was victor in the battle" when he means that the Romans won; conversely, Cicero in a letter to Brutus said "We have imposed on the people and are regarded as orators," when he is speaking only of himself. This sort of thing is not only an oratorical Ornament, but is acceptable usage in everyday speech (8.6.21).

Some people use Synecdoche, Quintilian continues, when "we grasp from the context something that is not actually expressed." Virgil writes "Arcades ad portas ruere" (the Arcadians, a rush to the gates), where the "historic infinitive," as the Loeb editor explains, is interpreted as an ellipse for *coepi* or *pergo*.

Du Marsais distinguishes synecdoche from its embarrassingly close neighbor metonymy by noting that if you say of someone who likes alcohol that he likes his bottle, that is simple metonymy, because the bottle isn't part of a whole, it's beside the alcohol or connected to it as a necessary delivery service, but if you say a hundred sails (*cent voiles*) where you mean a hundred ships (*cent vaisseaux*) that's synecdoche, because you have extended the normal meaning of *voiles*. In synecdoche, the part is always cited; not necessarily in metonymy, where besidedness is enough. Du Marsais proposes several branches of synecdoche: of genre; of kind (hard to separate these); of number (singular for plural, plural for singular); of part for whole, whole for part. But he keeps coming back to the difference between synecdoche and metonymy as if it were a pebble under his foot. Fontanier spends most of his commentary on du Marsais's errors, as in mistaking synecdoche for antonomasia once, for catachresis a little later, and for metonymy several times. But he arrives at his own conclusion, that in some phrases metonymy and synecdoche are six of one, half a dozen of the other.

Metaphor

We normally—and justly—speak of metaphor as an irruption of desire, specifically the desire to transform life by reinterpreting it, giving it a different story. The proper, straightforward meaning

of a force is fine—no, all right, if not quite fine—and it is mostly
what we live on, but if it were entirely sufficient, metaphor and the
other figures would not exist; there would be no call for them. We
need them because ordinary, proper meanings are not enough,
and so far as they coincide with their official objects, the coin-
cidings are complacent as they sink into themselves. We have, in
metaphor, the possibility of seeing those proper meanings glori-
ously enhanced, thrown aloft into grand affiliations, as when Hart
Crane invokes "adagios of islands" and "the seal's wide spindrift
gaze toward paradise," we feel in the blood the thrill of "new
thresholds, new anatomies."

But suppose someone, perhaps a man dressed all in black, sits on
a park bench, and shares nothing of these desires and fulfillments.
Is not thrilled by "adagios of islands." Sits apart among proper
meanings, and finds no joy in them. He might be Kafka on December 6, 1921, writing in his diary to keep from doing nothing:

> December 6. From a letter: "During this dreary winter I warm
> myself by it." Metaphors are one among many things which
> make me despair of writing. Writing's lack of independence of
> the world, its dependence on the maid who tends the fire, on
> the cat warming itself by the stove; it is even dependent on the
> poor old human being warming himself by the stove. All these
> are independent activities ruled by their own laws; only writ-
> ing is helpless, cannot live in itself, is a joke and a despair.[25]

He should have been a composer or a painter, independent of
maids, cats, and stoves, independent of metaphors, which can't
happen until maids, cats, and stoves cry to be freed from themselves and given new forms of life. At this point, metaphors encounter the fact that they depend on the poor old commonplaces

of life and can't live without them. The vehicle depends on the tenor that it transcends. Irony is the most sustained, the most unsympathetic, form of this dependence.

Irony

Irony begins when someone hearing a fable says, "No, I don't believe it; it's a lie." The ironist is alert to the difference between literal and figurative statements, and gives her support to the literal. She is against metaphor and other figures. She gets a reputation for being worldly, and for bringing common sense to bear on judgments and prejudices.

Fontanier is not much help. He says that "L'Ironie consiste à dire par une raillerie, ou plaisante, ou sérieuse, le contraire de ce qu'on pense, ou de ce qu'on veut faire penser."[26] But irony is not saying the opposite of what one thinks, it is saying exactly what one thinks, but in a quietly dissenting or derisory tone. Suppose there is a conversation in which each participant is playing the ball back, quite agreeably, to her friend. Then one of them says something. The other might object, storm off the court. But she doesn't. She dissents by changing the tone of the conversation, smiles without smiling, twists her voice to indicate that she is no longer playing her friend's game. Quietly, she disclaims her friend's idiom. Suppose her friend said: "The trouble with the working class is that they don't want to work," and the other answers, "Well, if they had honorable jobs, they would work hard enough." That would not be irony, because the conversation proceeds without change of tone. But if she answered by saying, "I love the way you say things; so quaint. I've always found your voice charming." That would be irony, because the second speaker steps aside from an ostensibly serious conversation and disowns its convention. She talks as if they were playing styles. Or as if she were a skeptic, for the moment, answering the naïveté of her friend. The ironist, as Kierkegaard described him, is supercilious, superior to those he condescends to speak to. His first purpose is—in this like the metaphorist—"to feel free," his second—I might add—is to enjoy the embarrassment he inflicts on his friend.[27] When, in Shakespeare's *Tempest,* Miranda exclaims, seeing Ferdinand and Alonso embrace, "O brave new world, / That has such people in't!," Prospero takes a moment of irony to say, possibly as an aside, " 'Tis new to thee" (V.1.185). Proust writes, in *Du Côté du chez Swann,* that sometimes, in spite of everything, Swann would let himself go so far as to express a judgment of a work of art, or of someone's sense of life, but then he would give his words an ironic tone as though he did not altogether associate himself with what he was saying. . . . "comme 'il n'adhérait pas tout entire à ce qu'il disait."[28]

Quintilian is more helpful than Fontanier: "Irony is that figure of speech or trope in which something contrary to what is said is to be understood" (contrarium ei quod dicitur intelligendum est) (9.22.44). Most of the theorists of irony look back to the passages in the *Nicomachean Ethics* where Aristotle distinguishes between three types of behavior: the boastful type who plays up his own truth (this is the *alazon*), the self-deprecating type (the *eiron,* a sly devil who goes in for mock-modesty), and the man who "attains the mean" and is "trustful in word and deed" (IV.7). This third man avoids metaphor if he can, especially in discursive and philosophic contexts. The vehicle of metaphor tends to fly high, making the most of its subject. The *eiron* stays on the ground; his favorite figure is *litotes,* keeping everything small. Cicero redeemed the *eiron* from any sinister connotations, and gave us the modern meaning, irony as civilized behavior, close to intelligent jesting.[29] Vico says that irony could not have begun until the period of reflection, because "it is fashioned of falsehood by dint of a reflection which wears the mask of truth" (II. 408). He confirms the sense that irony comes late in the civilized day; it is the figure of afterwords, of willful discrepancy. The ironist is most effective when he makes fun of the *alazon,* ridiculing his pomp and circumstance. In literature, the *eiron* is mainly a satirist, but sometimes—as in Jane Austen—she likes to subdue her ferocity to irony. Austen's irony impels her to keep her violence under restraint by staying at a distance from her subjects: she gives the impression that she is not ordaining the actions, and that the fate of her characters is out of her hands. She is merely reporting what society—or rather, English middle-class rural society—has already determined. The ironist is "neutral discoverer and explorer of incongruities."[30]

My favorite elucidations of irony come from H. W. Fowler, as one might expect:

> Irony is a form of utterance that postulates a double audience, consisting of one party that hearing shall hear and shall not understand, and another party that, when more is meant than meets the ear, is aware both of that more and of the outsiders' incomprehension.[31]

These three include Socratic irony—his profession of ignorance—dramatic irony, and the "irony of fate." Fowler ends his note:

> The above is an attempt to link intelligibly together three special senses of the word *irony,* which in its more general sense may be defined as the use of words intended to convey one meaning to the uninitiated part of the audience and another

to the initiated, the delight of it lying in the secret intimacy set up between the latter and the speaker; it should be added, however, that there are dealers in irony for whom the initiated circle is not of outside hearers, but is an *alter ego* dwelling in their own breasts.[32]

These understandings of irony may be brought again into relation with Kierkegaard's sense of irony—a far more elaborate concept. Socrates is the most thoroughgoing exemplar of Kierkegaard's irony. What Socrates valued most highly, Kierkegaard says, was "to stand still and come to himself."[33] To do this, he embodied "the subjective freedom which at every moment has within its power the possibility of a beginning and is not generated from previous conditions." It is as if, in my terms, the ironist enjoyed in himself the freedom we ascribe to metaphor, except that metaphor has to start from the literal sense and presence of the word even to fly freely beyond it. The freedom the ironist enjoys is absolute, in the sense that it directs itself "not against this or that particular existence but against the whole given actuality of a certain time and situation": "It is not this or that phenomenon but the totality of existence which it considers *sub specie ironiae*. To this extent one sees the propriety of the Hegelian characterization of irony as infinite absolute negativity."

The ironist's only purpose is to feel free in his subjectivity. As a figure of speech, Kierkegaard's irony looks down "on plain and ordinary discourse immediately understood by everyone; it travels in an exclusive incognito, as it were, and looks down from its exalted station with compassion on ordinary pedestrian speech." On the other hand: "Irony is free, to be sure, free from all the cares of actuality, but free from its joys as well, free from its blessings. For if it has nothing higher than itself, it may receive no blessing, for it is ever the lesser that is blessed of a greater. This is the freedom for which irony longs. It therefore keeps watch over itself, and fears nothing so much as that one or another impression may overwhelm it."[34]

It is impossible, therefore, to call on Kierkegaard's ironist to curb the excesses of metaphor—if you feel it is excessive in its freedom—on behalf of straightforward, plain statement: he scorns that just as much. For literal statements, if we want them, we have to rely on the privilege of common usage. That too includes metaphor and oxymoron, it doesn't take dictation from the given appearances.

If you want to take the wind out of the sails of metaphor, you need a more conventional kind of irony than Kierkegaard's. Arviragus, in Shakespeare's *Cymbeline,* sings a dirge, an aria, over the apparent corpse of Imogen:

> With fairest flowers
> Whilst summer lasts and I live here, Fidele,
> I'll sweeten thy sad grave: thou shalt not lack
> The flower that's like thy face, pale primrose, nor
> The azur'd harebell, like thy veins, no, nor
> The leaf of eglantine, whom not to slander,
> Out-sweet'ned not thy breath: the ruddock would,
> With charitable bill,—O bill, sore shaming
> Those rich-left heirs that let their fathers lie
> Without a monument!—bring thee all this;
> Yea, and furr'd moss besides, when flow'rs are none,
> To winter-ground thy corse.

It is beautiful in its way: the strewing of flowers on a grave is even now an appropriate, well-understood gesture. Perhaps the elabo-

rate parenthesis—O bill, sore shaming—is too much for the occasion. Guiderius interrupts his brother:

> Prithee, have done;
> And do not play in wench-like words with that
> Which is so serious. (IV.ii.218–231)

It is a severe rebuke, especially "play," "wench-like," and "serious."
But the most severe part of it is the rejection of the high style of
simile and metaphor.

The vernacular depends upon those severities to enforce its
value as the agreed middle style of conversation among equals.
The value arises from the fact that such language, by being social,
is irrefutably human. Stanley Cavell is right to say that common
or literal speech needs to be considered just as seriously as metaphor and other figures. (I'll quote him later). But it is possible to
withhold assent from common usage and the values it enforces. In
that case, one might even have the appearance of accepting these,
and that appearance would be an irony. Walter Pater describes
Marius the Epicurean in this esoteric condition:

> He was become aware of the possibility of a large dissidence
> between an inward and somewhat exclusive world of vivid
> personal apprehension, and the unimproved, unheightened re-
> ality of the life of those about him. As a consequence, he was
> ready now to concede, somewhat more easily than others, the
> first point of his new lesson, that the individual is to himself
> the measure of all things, and to rely on the exclusive certainty
> to himself of his own impressions. To move afterwards in that
> outer world of other people, as though taking it at their esti-
> mate, would be possible henceforth only as a kind of irony.[35]

But what is this "outer world of other people" and how does it speak?

Much of its speech is the demotic of a class or classes: on TV, *The Wire* gave these a good run. Securely middle-class people speak more decorously, on the whole, though it has become common for them to use the demotic for casual emphasis and to show that they are not immured in refinement. Hard to say how much of their idiolects started out as metaphor and have been forgotten in that character. Some philosophers of language think that all middle-class idiom is metaphorical at bottom. Bottom is a long way down, but in some cases we can fathom it precisely. Nate Silver wrote, in a recent issue of the *New York Times Magazine*: "In Michigan, Romney's opposition to the auto bailout may be too much of an albatross."[36] Every reader knows what Silver meant: a burden of guilt around his neck. But not every reader knows how that meaning has come about. The albatross, a large sea fowl, had no sinister or burdensome association till 1798 when Coleridge wrote "The Ancient Mariner" and had the sailors vent their rage against the Ancient, who has shot the albatross, by hanging the dead bird around his neck. "Instead of the cross, the Albatross / About my neck was hung." Coleridge's albatross entered into common English, was remembered for a while, then forgotten— Coleridge's poem too, forgotten—but it continued to be used for its reference, a sleeping metaphor unobtrusively active in the vernacular. How this metaphor awoke from its slumber, I can't say. Maybe Seidel's "seagulls flying their cries" will catch on, and compel the recognitions they precede.

Not Quite against Metaphor

For we perceive many things by the intellect for which language has no terms, a fact which Plato indicates plainly enough in his books by the employment of metaphors; for he perceived many things by the light of the intellect which everyday language was inadequate to express. (Multa namque per intellectum videmus, quibus signa vocalia desunt quod satis Plato insinuat in suis libris per assumptionem metaphorismorum; multa enim per lumen intellectuale vidit que sermone proprio nequivit exprimere.)

—Dante

Ordinary language breaks down in extraordinary cases. (In such cases, the cause of the breakdown is semantical.) Now no doubt an *ideal* language would *not* break down, whatever happened. In doing physics, for example, where our language is tightened up in order precisely to describe complicated and unusual cases concisely, we *prepare linguistically for the worst*. In ordinary language we do not: *words fail us*. If we talk as though an ordinary must be like an ideal language, we shall misrepresent the facts. . . . Ordinary language *blinkers* the already feeble imagination.

—J. L. Austin

> Metaphors are much more tenacious than facts.
>
> —Paul de Man

*O*n December 6, 1921, Franz Kafka, reading to himself a short sentence from a light-hearted letter he had recently written to his friend Robert Klopstock—"Ich wärme mich daran in diesem traurigen Winter (During this dreary winter I warm myself from this)"[1]—commented in his diary (I repeat):

> Metaphors are one among many things that make me despair of writing. Writing's lack of independence of the world, its dependence on the maid who tends the fire, on the cat warming itself by the stove; it is even dependent on the poor old human being warming himself by the stove. All these are independent activities ruled by their own laws; only writing is helpless, cannot live in itself, is a joke and a despair.[2]

But metaphors are not in a worse position than any other constituent of writing, except that they are supposed to testify to freedom, while the plain style is not. Denotation is expected to take dictation from the external world, so far as that can be acknowledged. Metaphor is supposed to imagine other worlds than this one, or at least other aspects of this one. But the difference between metaphor and ordinary language is not absolute. English is only English, German only German. Kafka's novels and stories are written in a common style that seems to be saturnine on principle. It's as if Kafka knew all the capacities of German but had no time for them, no confidence in them. He seems to be writing under duress, as if he would regard eloquence as a crime. In these fictions, horrific events are delivered in a deadpan style: a grocer might be counting his takings. His fiction is a "mourning play"—a *trauerspiel*—a collection of allegories, such that I recall Walter Benjamin's distinction between allegory and symbol:

> Whereas in the symbol destruction is idealized and the transfigured face of nature is fleetingly revealed in the light of redemption, in allegory the observer is confronted with the *facies hippocratica* of history as a petrified, primordial landscape. Everything about history that, from the very beginning, has been untimely, sorrowful, unsuccessful, is expressed in a face—or rather in a death's head.[3]

But there is a further consideration. Kafka takes the freedom of metaphor not by searching among the verbal figures but by imagining different forms of life. The philosopher Thomas Nagle has published an essay called "What Is It Like to Be a Bat?" He doesn't mean: what would it be like for me to become a bat? He means: what is it like for a bat to be a bat? My answer has to be: I have no idea. But Kafka achieved structural or narrative metaphors by asking himself what it is like for a dog to be a dog, a mouse to be a mouse, a large bug—or whatever it is—to be itself, an anonymous little animal, in "The Burrow," to be an anonymous little animal, maybe a badger? Kafka doesn't know the answers, either, but he can enter far enough into the imagining of such bizarreries that he discovers weirdnesses like the "beast" imagined by the small animal in that story. These are metaphors of a kind. Even my "bizarreries" depend to some extent on Walter Bagehot's reference to "the bizarreries of Mr. Dickens's genius." The unspoken question for Kafka was what is it like to be Franz Kafka, redemption in Benjamin's sense being out of the question?

As for the autonomy that Kafka attributes to the maid tending the fire, the cat warming itself by the stove, the man or woman by the stove, he exaggerates. These acts, if they are acts, are not spontaneous. If I warm myself by the stove on a wintry morning, it is because I've seen someone else do the same thing and I want to be sociable. I depend upon the examples of other people as much as a word in English depends upon other words in English. Autonomy is rare.

In 1985 the journal *Salmagundi* published an essay by Robert Mankin called "A Introduction to [Stanley Cavell's] *The Claim of Reason*." Cavell's book had appeared in 1979, so Mankin had plenty of time to examine it. His essay is probing, careful, judicious. Approaching Cavell's relation to the institution of language, Mankin notes "Cavell's identification of the human project with convention and normality and purposiveness of the most general sort." This leads him to question Cavell's sense of words:

> *Chair* and *Stuhl* and *kathedra* all refer to the "same" institution but their modes of doing so create large differences between them. In a particular mother tongue—for Cavell, it doesn't matter which one—the universality of human convention reaches to expression. The individual character of each signifier and its differing figurative possibilities serve, or at least do not hamper, this expression. Yet Cavell professes to have left the problem of figurative language untouched. This surprising avowal—is metaphor less essential to language than its generality?—points to the same double sense of convention. After learning particular words and forms of life, we project them in ways we learn to consider "natural." Metaphor has

no place in this account, for Cavell, because it is always conceived as (at least slightly) "unnatural."[4]

Mankin thinks this distinction between the natural and the unnatural questionable for several reasons:

> Since *human* nature, social projection, are at issue here rather than nature as such, the only criterion for what is natural (or normal) is its intelligibility in my world, its capacity to be accommodated by a grammar; also because "unnatural," as [Cavell] uses it, means forced, and we have seen that force does not disappear from the role of human convention either. Cavell may be reserved about discussing figurative language just to the extent that it points to the forcing element (and generality) in all convention. Things which the child naturally comes to know, for instance that stepping on a crack will lead to someone splitting, that "guilt" can follow sleeping in a bed or sitting in someone's chair: these may be the most unnatural and figurative expressions of all. The most deeply social of experiences may thus transcend our human forms of life and deserve other names like myth or literature or psychosis.[5]

Mankin had several other points to make about Cavell's recourse to philosophy and literature, the natural and the unnatural, use and force, but we may let them stand.

Cavell replied to Mankin's essay in "Postscript C: The Skeptical and the Metaphorical," an appendix to his *In Quest of the Ordinary: Lines of Skepticism and Romanticism* (1988). He had a good deal to say about other issues, but eventually came to the main dispute:

> Mankin asks at one point: "Is metaphor less essential to language than its generality?" as though I had rather suggested

that metaphor was indeed less essential. His question is prompted by my discussion of what I call projecting a word, in chapter 7 ("Excursus on Wittgenstein's Vision of Language") of *The Claim of Reason*. I do not find my discussion to devalue metaphor's essentiality. The discussion is meant to gloss Wittgenstein's implied attack in [on?] traditional philosophical "explanations" of the generality of language which invoke what were called "universals." Mankin says of the discussion: "Metaphor has no place in this account, for Cavell, because it is always conceived as . . . 'unnatural.'" But in ending my chapter with the thought that metaphorical "transfer" is, in contrast with nonmetaphorical "projection," aptly describable as unnatural, I rather imagined that making, or showing, metaphor's "place" in language is just what I was about. It is true that the moral of this passage is that the metaphorical is implicitly shunned as an explanation of the generality of language; but this is hardly a slighting of the metaphorical, since my claim is that nothing (philosophical) will constitute such an explanation. Nor does it follow from this that the metaphorical is not "essential" to what we think of as language.[6]

But in the next paragraph Cavell gives other reasons:

If I am reserved about discussing figurative language in *The Claim of Reason,* the cause is more immediately, I would say, my dissatisfaction with the identifications and theories of figurative language that I have come across, and perhaps above all with my sense that the importance of the figurative in those theories seems somehow to go without saying, as if it held the key to language, to literariness, to the (destructive) ambitions of philosophy, etc. Perhaps the figurative strikes me as of no more importance than whatever it is supposed to exist in contrast with, say, the literal.[7]

As if these sentences were not enough, Cavell juxtaposes two "ways":

> It is part of the sense of the unavoidability of both routes of the unnatural (up to metaphor, down to skepticism) that neither requires expertise. And this is part of the sense that both routes are natural to the human, all but inescapable for creatures with the capacity to converse, to subject themselves to intelligibility, to make themselves readable. But there is this apparent difference between the routes, that one *can* get along in the everyday world without exercising the capacity for the figurative, while one can *only* get along in that world (can only "have" that world) if one does *not* exercise the capacity to [for?] skepticism. This latter absence will deprive you of access to certain philosophical fears and ambitions; the former absence will debar you from certain other intimacies.[8]

What those intimacies are, or might be, Cavell does not say, but I hope that a sense of them or of their fellows may have emerged occasionally from the book in your hands.

The issue between Michael Mankin and Stanley Cavell turns indeed on a question of "ordinary language" and figurative language. Sensitive as Cavell is to the incorrigible ambiguity of ordinary language, nonetheless he holds that it deserves its prestige because it is the language through which children learn to talk. Metaphor, he thinks, is no good for that purpose. Glossing Wittgenstein's observation in the *Blue Book* that "we learn words in *certain* contexts," Cavell takes this to mean "both that we do not learn words in *all* the contexts in which they could be used (what, indeed, would that mean?) and that not every context in which a word is used is one in which the word *can* be learned (e.g., contexts in which the word is used metaphorically)."[9] An instance I draw from Shakespeare's *Twelfth Night*. If you didn't already know the range of meanings of the word "natural" and a certain meaning of the word "perspective," you wouldn't make much of, or learn anything from, Orsino's saying, when Sebastian enters near the end of the play,

> One face, one voice, one habit, and two persons—
> A natural perspective that is and is not. (V.i. 211–212)

But the passage that got Cavell into most serious trouble with Mankin is this one from *The Claim of Reason:*

> The phenomenon I am calling "projecting a word" is the fact of language which, I take it, is sometimes responded to by saying that "All language is metaphorical." Perhaps one could say: the possibility of metaphor is the same as the possibility of language generally, but what is essential to the projection of a word is that it proceeds, or can be made to proceed, *naturally;* what is essential to a functioning metaphor is that its "transfer" is *unnatural*—it breaks up the established, normal direction of projection.[10]

Even with the italics, to call this distinction one between the natural and the unnatural has little merit. True, if you are reading a sentence and you suddenly meet a metaphor, you may feel that you are being made to leap out of your standing: "We sat in his dark crowded room at the boarding house. An ironing board stood unfolded at the window. There were chipped enamel pots, trays of utensils set on a dresser. The furniture was vague, foundling."[11] "Foundling"? I leap out of my chair, run to the OED. Foundling: "a deserted infant whose parents are unknown, a child whom there is no one to claim." Well, yes. Then figuratively, from 1587, "as for lying or untruth, it is a foundling, and not a thing bred." Figuratively from 1853: "The great majority of proverbs are foundlings, the happier foundlings of a nation's wit." De Lillo's "vague" is on a different level than "foundling," but there is no merit in calling one natural and the other unnatural; both are cultural, the difference must be described within culture. Cavell thinks of metaphor as a scandal because it "breaks up the established, normal direction of projection." Projection too is assimilated to the norms of ordinary language. But "established" and "normal" have little traction; they are not self-evident.

Mankin made the issues between himself and Cavell clear, or clear enough, and he forced Cavell to be more explicit than he regularly cares to be. So much to the good. I agree with Cavell that the primacy, the privileging of metaphor, is too often allowed to go without saying. It is a complication that what he calls "the literal" is rampant with metaphors new and old, awake and sleeping, and that those impurities can't be excised. It is not surprising that theorists of the vernacular find they have intractable materials to deal with. My own interest is in aspects, as if a boy were turning a globe in his hands, alert to one image—call it that, provisionally—while he waited for the next. He would not care about repetitions; he would trust that the aspects would each appear a little different, catching a different light.

I take it that "ordinary language"—if we concede its existence— is the way educated speakers of a language, English for example, talk when they are not involved in technical or high-brow discussions. I don't know whether or not Cavell includes, in his thinking about "the literal," such extravagances as street talk or gang talk, the kind of speech that Harriet Sergeant illuminates in *Among the Hoods: My Years with a Teenage Gang*. Probably not: there are limits. I doubt too that his sense of ordinary language includes the most potent version of it in our culture, the language of TV sitcoms. There is no need to assume that the literal, in a respectable sense, has entirely gone without saying: many philosophers, as Cavell well knows, have spent most of their professional lives thinking, talking, and writing about it: among them Wittgenstein, Ayer, Price, Austin, Ryle, Strawson, Warnock, Hampshire, and Searle. A survey of that "tradition" in modern philosophy would report a few agreements and many dissents among those philosophers on questions of usage and meaning. And many questions one wouldn't have thought of asking.

If you read Austin's *Philosophical Papers* along with his *Sense and Sensibilia* and *How to Do Things with Words,* you find him engaged with such questions as these: When is an utterance true? How do you know that Tom is angry? How do you know that this rose is red? What is a fact? What counts as an excuse? What does *If* mean? What is the difference between "I know" and "I believe"? What is the point of pretending? What is the difference, if any, between a performative and a constative utterance? What does the word "real" mean? Is there a difference between "precisely" and "exactly"? Are there any differences among "intentionally," "deliberately," and "on purpose"? Many ambitious philosophers would regard most of these questions as trivial, the small change of pragmatism, but Austin did not. Taking them seriously, he regularly produced as evidence for his position the testimony of common usage: he respected "the inherited experience and acumen of many

generations of men." He never offered as evidence the language
that issues from intuitions of the sublime, the poetic, the apoca-
lyptic, madness, hyperbole, the mathematical, mysticism, or skepticism. His standard position was this one:

> It must be added, too, that superstition and error and fantasy
> of all kinds do become incorporated in ordinary language
> and even sometimes stand up to the survival test (only, when
> they do, why should we not detect it?). Certainly, then, ordi-
> nary language is *not* the last word: in principle it can every-
> where be supplemented and improved upon and superseded.
> Only remember, it *is* the *first* word.[12]

Cavell's own work is largely a set of meditations on Shakespeare, Emerson, Thoreau, Poe, and Beckett with Austin and
Wittgenstein constantly in mind. Like Austin, he acknowledges
the privilege of common usage, or at least the usage of the common room. But he counsels against taking Austin easily or taking
"ordinary language" as if its implied way were already achieved:
"The phrase 'ordinary language' is, of course, of no special interest; the problem is that its use has so often quickly suggested that
the answers to the fundamental questions it raises, or ought to
raise, are known, whereas they are barely imagined."[13] Austin's
"fundamental philosophical interest," according to Cavell, lay
"in drawing distinctions," but he didn't remark that Austin often
pursued his distinctions to the point of undermining them: he
seemed quite sanguine when he had proved himself wrong. He
undermined the distinction he was foremost in making between
performative and constative utterances, for example, by concluding that both categories were examples of "speech acts." It is not
clear why he did not maintain distinctions, even then, among

different forms of speech acts. Metaphor, I hasten to remark, is not a device for drawing distinctions. It has no interest in doing so. It is a device for colonizing new thresholds, new anatomies, monsters, and dinosaurs. In *How to Do Things with Words* Austin rules out of his account words spoken by an actor on a stage, the words of a poem, and words spoken in a soliloquy. These are not allowed to confound his main or official interests. They "fall under the doctrine of the *etiolations* of language."[14] This charge is harsh if it means what it says, Austin's italics included. *Etiolation* means "blanching," a condition in which a plant becomes colorless by being deprived of light. Applied to language, *etiolations* is a metaphor, but Austin holds, in an aristocratic tone, that a decent norm of speech is fulfilled when a man of sound mind says something that may be important in a language he knows well enough to be understood. He had no interest in flute-playing centaurs. How a metaphor could be deemed to be a feeble or blanched form of ordinary language, or how there could be a doctrine of etiolations, I can't say. But it is clear that Austin was against metaphor at least to the extent of regarding it as beside the normal point.

I have no further reason to think that Austin deplored metaphor or even that he thought the metaphorical capacity a damned nuisance. It would be a nuisance only if it interfered with his duty as a teacher of philosophy, fellow of an Oxford college, instructing his pupils how to do proper things with proper words in conventional circumstances. Derrida rebuked him for setting aside metaphor, stage speeches, poems, and soliloquies from his consideration of communication. He maintained that if Austin were to take these "infelicities" seriously as problems in his theory, the theory would collapse.[15] But Austin is entitled to be prudent and to set the limits of his consideration wherever he thinks they should hold: his decisions are obviously strategic. Why Cavell is unforthcoming about metaphors and other figures is harder to say: the authors (and films) he writes about are rich in metaphors, but he has found ways of discussing them—mostly in terms of moral or immoral behavior—without emphasizing their figures of speech. He seems content to divine his profundities by rattling the cage of ordinary language. He doesn't begin with opacity.

Stanley Fish raised a provocative question: "How ordinary is ordinary language?" Before answering it, he enlarged the context by considering the disputes between linguists and literary critics: "Linguists resolutely maintain that literature is, after all, language, and that therefore a linguistic description of a text is necessarily relevant to the critical act; critics just as resolutely maintain that linguistic analyses leave out something, and that what they leave out is precisely what constitutes literature."[16] Linguists and literary critics agree on "the positivist assumption that ordinary language is available to a purely formal description." This agreement is fruitless, "for if one begins with an impoverished notion of ordinary language, something that is then defined as a deviation from ordinary language will be doubly impoverished." Fish contends that the very act of distinguishing between ordinary and literary language, because of what it assumes, leads necessarily to an inadequate account of both . . . *"deviation theories always trivialize the norm and therefore trivialize everything else"* (his italics).

Fish argues that *"there is no such thing as ordinary language* [again, his italics] at least in the naïve sense intended by that term: an abstract formal system, which, in John Searle's words, is only used incidentally for purposes of human communication."[17] Fish then moves to align himself, it appears, with Austin and other Oxford philosophers who hold, in their theory of speech acts, that "the language system is not characterized apart from the realm of value and intention, but begins and ends with that realm." What this gives us is "a continuum of speech acts no one of which can claim primacy." A theory "which restores human content to language also restores legitimate status to literature by reuniting it with a norm that is no longer trivialized." On a second thought, Fish then asserts that "there is no norm," since the inclusive continuum makes it unnecessary to have one. Literature "is no longer granted a special status, but since that special status has always been implicitly degrading, this disadvantage is finally literature's greatest gain."

The first problem with the continuum, I think, is that we must be prepared to say that anything and everything in language is six of one and half a dozen of the other. My saying "Good morning, Jack" then becomes the same as—at least thrown into the same bin as—Horatio's saying to Marcellus and Barnardo, "But look, the morn in russet mantle clad / Walks o'er the dew of yon high eastward hill." Mine is just as much a speech act as Horatio's. It would be desirable for some purposes to distinguish them, but how? If you put into the continuum anything that takes a verbal form, how can you pick out something and say that it's literature? How can I choose a word or a phrase and say that it's a metaphor, if Fish has forbidden me to talk of it as a deviation from a norm? Fish deals with the first question—what is literature?—by saying that literature "is language around which we have drawn a frame, a frame that indicates a decision to regard with a particular self-consciousness the resources language has always possessed." He should have said "I" rather than "we," unless he claims that the frame is socially spontaneous, but in that case, whose "self-consciousness" is operative? How has "I" become "we"? Fish's device of framing certain words is open to all the problems entailed by "inside" and "outside" or by the rejected norm his frame brings back. If the particular words are framed, they are distinguished, invidiously, from all the words that are not in the frame. So a difference is inevitable, whether we call it a deviation or not. If I want to mark a difference between my speech act and Horatio's—since they are evidently not "the same" to me—Fish has simply kicked the difference, as a problem, down the road. Similarly with metaphor, which is palpably different from the words that accompany it, as in an ordinary sentence. Fish says further: "What characterizes literature then is not formal properties, but an attitude—always within our power to assume—toward properties that belong by constitutive right to language." (This raises the intriguing possibility that literary language may be the norm, and message-bearing language a device we carve out to perform the special, but certainly not normative, task of imparting information.)[18] Shall I assume what Fish assumes? If not, the disagreement in incorrigible. Besides, no one has ever confined "ordinary language" to the task of imparting information. Austin's sense of "how to do things with words" is much wider than that. Fish again: "Literature is still a category, but it is an open category, not definable by fictionality, or by a disregard of propositional truth, or by a statistical predominance of tropes and figures, but simply by what we decide to put into it. The difference lies not in the language, but in ourselves."[19] Fish does not indicate what it is "we decide to put into it." He appears to claim: any sequence of words is literature—a poem or a novel—if I say it is. If so, the category is more open than I want it to be. Fish continues: "One obvious difficulty with this view is that it contains no room for evaluation. It can, however, explain the *fact* of evaluating by pointing out that the formal signals which trigger the 'framing process' in the reader are also evaluative criteria. That is, they simultaneously *identify* 'literature' (by signaling the reader that he should put on his literary perceiving set; it is the reader who 'makes' literature) and *honors* (or validates) the piece of language so identified (i.e., made)." But "so identified" is not the same as "so made." I may identify *Paradise Lost* and call it a particular kind of poem, but I have not made it. All aesthetics, then, according to Fish, "are local and conventional rather than universal, reflecting a collective decision as to what will count as literature, a decision that will be in force only so long as a community of readers or believers (it is very much an act of faith) continues to abide by it." How such a decision goes from being individual—the decision of one man or woman of sound mind—to being collective and issuing from a community of readers, Fish does not say, either in this essay or in his books that argue for "reader-response" criticism. As for metaphor, personification, and other figures, I don't contest the view that Horatio's morn in russet mantle clad could walk into another sentence in Fish's open category. All I need to claim is the right to pay special attention to the way it walks, in *Hamlet,* o'er yon high eastward hill.

One of the standard arguments against metaphor is that it lures people into mistaking a metaphor for an entity, or for ordinary statement—the kind that Austin called "constative." This from Harold Bloom: "Our culture in all of its most frozen aspects has been created by its literalization of anterior tropes. Indeed, our concept of culture itself is such a literalization."[20] I wonder about this complaint. "Frozen" is itself a literalization of the figurative. Bloom may be saying: "It's a pity that a metaphor should die," but it is not like him to say anything so modest. The ease with which he refers to "our culture" allows me to think that the damage done by literalization is slight. The OED gives as the first meaning of "culture" husbandry, cultivation of the ground to produce crops and flowers. By an easy extension we come to cultivate our minds by thought and education. From there, we enhance a culture to include the arts. When a democratic spirit obtains, we say that a culture means all the social and other activities of a particular people living in a certain place. The literal sense came first, the figurative later. I have heard Mary Robinson assert, in a recent speech, that we should not use "culture" in this sense of community; we should reserve it for universal human rights. But that too has only the force of her office as UN commissioner for human rights. When a metaphor is new, there is no liability for error: those who advert to it recognize it for the novel thing it is and are careful in its presence. But when the metaphor has been in common speech for a long time, people forget its metaphorical character and start using it as part of the vernacular; they let their guard down. The vernacular is contaminated—or improved—by metaphors that are soon forgotten as metaphors and come to be used as ordinary speech. If Nietzsche is right, such metaphors soon become tokens of accepted truth. But "contaminated" may not be the right word: there may be no mischief at all when a metaphor becomes commonplace.

Hannah Arendt has maintained that when metaphors intrude upon scientific reasoning, "they are used and misused to create and provide plausible evidence for theories that are actually mere hypotheses that have to be proved or disproved by facts." Typically modern pseudosciences, such as psychoanalysis, "owe their plausibility to the seeming evidence of metaphor, which they substitute for the lacking evidence of data." Her prime example, taken from

Hans Blumenberg's *Paradigmen zu einer Metaphorologie,* is the theory
of consciousness in psychoanalysis, "where consciousness is seen as
the peak of an iceberg, a mere indication of the floating mass of
unconsciousness beneath it." This theory, Arendt argues, cannot be
demonstrated, because "the moment a fragment of unconsciousness reaches the peak of the iceberg, it has become conscious and
lost all the properties of its alleged origin." The metaphor, since it
is not an argument, precludes demonstration. Arendt further:

> Yet the evidence of the iceberg metaphor is so overwhelming
> that the theory needs neither argument nor demonstration;
> we would find the metaphor's use unobjectionable if we were
> told that we were dealing with speculations about something
> unknown—in the same way that former centuries used anal-
> ogies for speculations about God. The only trouble is that
> every such speculation carries with it a mental construct in
> whose systematic order every datum can find its hermeneutic
> place with an even more stringent consistency than that pro-
> vided by a successful scientific theory, since, being an exclu-
> sively mental construct without need of any real experience,
> it does not have to deal with exceptions to the rule.[21]

But this implies that a metaphor can't be judged or held to account. It is true that a metaphor gives every appearance of being
a spontaneous act of imagination; it seems to transcend reasons
and disputes. But it can be judged after the event.

Here are two troublesome cases. The narrator of *Middlemarch*
says, in Chapter 10: "Poor Mr Casaubon had imagined that his
long, studious bachelorhood had stored up for him a compound
interest of enjoyment and that large drafts on his affections would
not fail to be honoured; for we all of us, grave or light, get our

thoughts entangled in metaphors, and act fatally on the strength of them."[22] I agree that we often take metaphors literally, but I'm not convinced that as a result we get ourselves entangled in error and confusion. The metaphors we live by include ones we are driven by, and the consequences may be woeful. But the particular instance George Eliot's narrator gives, with an implication that one such is decisive, is unjust, and weak as evidence. This is the first we have heard of Casaubon's alleged habit of mind in his treatment of his associates. We know that he is a parson, well-off through inherited means and notably generous in his provision for his nephew Will Ladislaw. He is made to be a bachelor; it has been suggested that he is impotent.[23] He gives his life to scholarship, pursuing futile research toward a "Key to all Mythologies." If he had continued with this work, without turning aside to marry, his life would probably not have amounted to much, but he would have done no harm. He made the mistake of thinking that he should marry, and he instructed himself that he would find felicity in the company of a local girl, Dorothea Brooke. She made the equally serious mistake of thinking that Casaubon's treasure of knowledge would ensure her happiness. But I find only two sentences in preceding chapters that might raise a question about Casaubon's habit of mind and feeling in relation to other people. They come with his marriage proposal in a letter to Dorothea that is otherwise entirely decent: "To be accepted by you as your husband and the earthly guardian of your welfare, I should regard as the highest of providential gifts. In return, I can at least offer you an affection hitherto unwasted, and the faithful consecration of a life which, however short in the sequel, has no backward pages whereon, if you choose to turn them, you will find records such as might justly cause you either bitterness or shame."[24] "In return" is blunt, with its suggestion of "I'll give you this and then you'll give me that." Still, polite society regards giving a gift and receiving one "in turn" as entirely appropriate. In the rest of the letter, Casaubon is saying: my emotional life is an open book. Feel free to read it. You won't find any page of it that will distress you. I have not "wasted" my emotion on anyone. Clearly, none of these statements justifies the severities that lead up to the narrator's moral generalization.

To come to the narrator's thought on metaphor, marriage, supposedly, is money in the bank, especially if you already have plenty of it by having been a clean-living bachelor all these years. You can expect to draw large checks on your account and know that they will be fulfilled. That is what the words "stored," "compound interest," "large drafts on," and "honoured" add up to, if I may put it that way. The words together make an extended metaphor, issuing from "stored." "Unwasted" is prudential, "waste not, want not." But there is no indication, in *Middlemarch* up to this point, that Casaubon has thought or acted in this way or been driven by mercenary considerations. Of course he should have remained a bachelor all his life. And Dorothea should have curbed her reverence for knowledge and waited until "the right man" came along. But poor Casaubon, as the narrator calls him, did not regard Dorothea as money in the bank; nor is he shown as having the sensibility of a venture capitalist.

An even more famous sentence turns up in Chapter 20, where the narrator remarks that we are not deeply moved by the commonplaces of our experience:

> That element of tragedy which lies in the very fact of frequency, has not yet wrought itself into the coarse emotion of mankind; and perhaps our frames could hardly bear much of

it. If we had a keen vision and feeling of all ordinary human life, it would be like hearing the grass grow and the squirrel's heart beat, and we should die of that roar which lies on the other side of silence. As it is, the quickest of us walk about well wadded with stupidity.[25]

This is not as easy as it has appeared to some readers of *Middlemarch*. The first sentence seems to say, with its emphasis on "yet" and "coarse" and "perhaps our frames could hardly bear much of it," that it is our good fortune that we haven't learned to take our commonplaces tragically. If we did, our sensory experiences would be immensely exacerbated, "and we should die of that roar which lies on the other side of silence." What is that roar, and where is the other side of silence, and—if it comes to that—where is this side of silence? We are not likely to act fatally on the strength of our metaphors if we don't know what they are or what they portend. I agree with J. Hillis Miller that "the overt reference of the 'roar' is 'all ordinary human life.' "[26] But then he calls the roar by several invidious names—chaos, formlessness, death—and these have the effect of nullifying "ordinary human life." Such a life contains death, inevitably, but it gets by, keeps going while the going is good, by customs, habits, repetitions, little daily orders, waking and sleeping, all the things we do before dying, even if most of these are—as Adorno maintained—administered. If they are given by the metaphor "roar," it is not a metaphor we get entangled in or act fatally on the strength of. How does this roar "lie on the other side of silence"? If the roar is, at least to begin with, "all ordinary human life," then silence is the ultimate question: Why is there something rather than nothing?—Leibniz's question that George Eliot does not propose to answer. But I can't see myself acting fatally on the strength of this metaphor. I do the best I can under more immediate compulsions.

I can't think of myself as being entangled in metaphors, but I concede that I would be the last to know. The book to read in this connection is *Metaphors We Live By* by George Lakoff and Mark Johnson. They define a metaphor as *"understanding and experiencing one kind of thing in terms of another"* (their italics, p. 5). They maintain that "human *thought processes* are largely metaphorical" (p. 6). This seems to mean that most of the words we use in ordinary speech were once live metaphors and have lapsed in the vernacular, their metaphorical character quite forgotten but still, as Lakoff and Johnson claim, potent as the prime vehicle of thought in practice. The main example of this potency, in *Metaphors We Live By,* is "the conceptual metaphor ARGUMENT IS WAR." Think of what we say in arguing. "Your claims are *indefensible.* He *attacked every weak point* in my argument. His criticisms were *right on target.* I *demolished* his argument. I've never *won* an argument with him. You disagree? Okay, *shoot!* If you use that *strategy,* he'll *wipe you out.* He *shot down all* of my arguments." Lakoff and Johnson comment:

> It is important to see that we don't just *talk* about arguments in terms of war. We can actually win or lose arguments. We see the person we are arguing with as an opponent. We attack his positions and we defend our own. We gain and lose ground. We plan and use strategies. If we find one position indefensible, we can abandon it and take a new line of attack. Many of the things we *do* in arguing are partially structured by the concept of war. Though there is no physical battle, there is a verbal battle, and the structure of an argument—attack, defense,

counterattack, etc.—reflects this. It is in this sense that the AR-
GUMENT IS WAR metaphor is one that we live by in this
culture; it structures the actions we perform in arguing.[27]

These assertions are not entirely true. Wars end, if they do, in
peace, sometimes with formal treaties. Besides, there are many
people who never argue, on principle. Besides further, if rhetoric
is the art of persuasion, Jack may reach a point in the argument at
which he says: "Jill, I think you're right, I'll vote for Obama after
all, with some misgiving." Or he may call for a truce and say, "Let's
agree to differ." Or if John is Professor Austin leading a seminar in
an Oxford college, he will not think of it as an occasion for winning
or losing; he will take pleasure in the process, the time well spent,
of the discussion. True, Nietzsche denounced Socrates as a bully,
haranguing those beardless youths, and I have known teachers who
have enjoyed their reputations as curmudgeons. But I am impressed
by the number of words we use to describe the various forms in
which people talk, not all of them warlike: quarrel, row, challenge,
dispute, debate, discussion, seminar, conversation, chat, introspec-
tion, soliloquy, "the dialogue of the mind with itself." These differ
in tone; new metaphors govern their practice. As in athletics and
other sports, Roger Federer competes with Juan Martin del Potro
and at the end they hug, no matter who has won. Even with Andy
Murray there are smiles and handshakes. Chess games end in the
same way, or are supposed to. You are not supposed to win at tennis
by shooting your opponent.

Lakoff and Johnson don't stick to metaphors, they turn aside to
acknowledge, however briefly, some kindred terms, especially
personification, metonymy, and synecdoche. Personification occurs when a thing is described as if it were a person or an animal.

"His *theory explained* to me the behavior of chickens raised in fac-
tories. This *fact argues* against the standard theories. *Life has cheated*
me. *Inflation is eating up* our profits." Or my favorite personification,
John Fletcher's "Come Sleep and with thy sweet deceiving / Lock
me in delight a while." Metonymy, according to Lakoff and Johnson, is "the use of one entity to refer to another that is related to
it." Mrs. Grundy frowns on blue jeans = she frowns on the wearing
of blue jeans. Metonymy differs from metaphor, as I've already
remarked, by being a spatial figure: two things are placed—or
more often—found near each other; they make a relation—not
necessarily metaphorical—if someone thinks of them together.
They are like what Marshall McLuhan or someone else referred
to as "juxtaposition without copula," as in a painting where we are
not told how one point of interest is related—or may be related—
to another; no grammar or syntax leads us through the painting.
A metonymic relation is like alliteration in a poem: two words
that may be quite distant from each other are called together by
alliteration, and perhaps by that alone; it is up to every reader to
make something of the relation. But there is a stricter account of
metonymy, advanced by Brian Vickers, in which metonymy "involves the substitution of a 'related' term (where *propinquis* does
not mean literally 'next to') according to fixed transitions or trop-
ings within a category on different levels, such as putting the
container for the thing contained, or the sign for the thing signified."[28] Metonymy has been found productive in psychological
and psychoanalytic writings from Krafft-Ebing to Lacan because
questions of similarity and changes of identity don't arise. Instead,
there is Freudian displacement of one object to another, as in shoe
fetishism. In metaphor there is a transfer of energy from tenor
through vehicle; transfer is the essential factor, as Aristotle says.

Likenesses, however occult, tend to find their destiny in metaphor, but not always. The OED claims as synecdoche the use of part for whole, as when a warrior uses as an amulet parts of the skull of a slain foe. Lakoff and Johnson mention synecdoche as "a special case of metonymy," but they don't say how it is special. Vickers says it is "where one thing is substituted for another, part for whole, genus for species, and vice versa." He gives as an example Volumnia in Shakespeare's *Coriolanus:* "These are the ushers of Marcius: before him he carries noise, and behind him he leaves tears" (II.i.158).

I notice a feature of the metaphors Lakoff and Johnson say we live by: none of them is presented as sinister. The ARGUMENT IS WAR metaphor is the most dangerous, but there is no blood on the floor. Even if virtually every detail of ordinary speech is metaphorical, we don't seem to suffer or do any harm by this. Lakoff and Johnson haven't produced any metaphors in common speech that are noxious; they all seem to have been domesticated. I'm having difficulty finding metaphors in which my thoughts have been entangled and the effect is fatal. The only one I can think of is "move on," a plea made popular by President Clinton when he tried, successfully indeed, to retain his office. "It is time to move on," as if his predicament were that of some poor fellow who had slipped on an icy pavement and fallen hard. Of course he must pick himself up and move on; it's the only thing to do. What most people do, according to Lakoff and Johnson, seems pretty reasonable; there are no monsters at large, or even careless drivers. The book ends with a few (not many, not enough) pages on the philosophic position they favor: they call it experientialism and claim that it fulfills the reasonable demands made by the philosophies they reject, "subjectivism" and "objectivism." Specifically: "From the experientialist perspective, truth depends on understanding, which emerges from functioning in the world. It is through such understanding that the experientialist alternative meets the objectivist's need for an account of truth. It is through the coherent structuring of experience that the experientialist alternative satisfies the subjectivist's need for personal meaning and significance."[29] The moral of the story seems to be agreeable: what we do in the ordinary world with ordinary speech and deeds is all right, or at worst not bad. I find no tangles, no woeful effects. I wonder who started the real wars, caused global warming, fomented congenital hatred, and gave us an endangered planet.

A question that Lakoff and Johnson haven't raised: shouldn't we—or someone—resent the fact that, if Lakoff and Johnson are right, people deal with nearly every situation in their daily lives by spontaneous recourse to metaphors that linguists think of as dead? These metaphors lead a vigorous afterlife, without any fuss, in our ordinary speech. Should I not resent the fact, or at least be defensively gruff about it, that so much of what I think of as my conscious life is governed by a clutter of dead metaphors I have long since forgotten to think of as metaphors? I don't recall that they were ever metaphors. It could be said that there is nothing in *The Metaphors We Live By* that was not in Locke, Hobbes, Sprat, and others who inveighed against the alleged deceits of metaphor and often inveighed in metaphors.

Another argument against metaphor is that it is redundant, or may be redundant, if the thing, the *tenor,* is already complete, such that a further enhancement by metaphor would be too much. Stevens, in a passage of "Bouquet of Roses in Sunlight" that I will quote again, says as much:

Say that it is a crude effect, black reds,
Pink yellows, orange whites, too much as they are
To be anything else in the sunlight of the room,

Too much as they are to be changed by metaphor,
Too actual, things that in being real
Make any imaginings of them lesser things.

Further down:

Our sense of these things changes and they change,
Not as in metaphor, but in our sense
Of them. So sense exceeds all metaphor.[30]

This is irrefutable, but only if we take Stevens's word for it that anything metaphor can do, sense can do better. If sense is the most extreme act of consciousness, or say of the creative imagination, we concede that it can do anything the mind can do and comprehend every figure in the rhetorician's book. But it will probably be found that in trying to describe the furthest reach of the imagination, we shall come upon metaphors even if we note their supersession. So Stevens's assertion is more a claim for the imagination than a dismissal of metaphor as a lesser thing.

Most of the commentaries on metaphor that I have seen are according to Aristotle and take for granted his claim that the command of metaphor is first proof of genius. The ability to see likeness where it is not evident—not evident to ordinary intelligences, that is—is the greatest gift. At that extreme point, the gleaned likeness becomes a new thing, a transformation of the original; it gives it a new character, like "marsupial" in Heaney's poem. In language, the transformation is accomplished by the transfer of a word or a phrase from its natural position in the language to an improper position elsewhere. The value of a metaphor seems to consist in the audacity of the transfer, the determination on the part of the writer to set new possibilities astir. The imagination that seizes these new possibilities in a language is the supreme capacity; call it Shakespeare. The power it exerts is free, unsponsored. It acts without permission. It is not the consequence of any circumstance that has preceded it. It is the *sprezzatura* of a language. This is according to Aristotle, or at least in his spirit.

Why would anyone disapprove of such freedom, unless—like Lakoff and Johnson—she thinks that metaphors drive people wild, beyond their reasonable behaviors? It is true that the vehicle of a metaphor enjoys its freedom, doesn't ask permission of its tenor, leaves the poor thing standing helpless, pays no attention to the privilege of usage, goes its own way. Inevitably, a writer with a Puritan streak in his sensibility would turn up, exclaiming that he would have no more cakes and ale—Robbe-Grillet, to be specific, who threatened that he would put a stop to adjectives and metaphors, the accretions, accessories that the culture has added to the proper, ascetic word.

Some modern critics have spoken "against metaphor." Two or three swallows don't make a summer, but these birds are formidable. I think of Gérard Genette who undertook to show "that many of the Proustian 'metaphors' are in fact metonymies or at least metaphors based on metonymies."[31] Genette resents the fact that so many critics—he names Michel Deguy, Jacques Sojcher, and the Liège Group—have inflated—as it seems to him—the significance of metaphor as "the trope of tropes," "the figure of figures," "the central figure of all rhetoric." He notes, with dismay, "the pro-

found desire of a whole modern poetics . . . to establish the absolute, undivided rule of metaphor."[32] Not that he is surprised. He
observes that as early as the sixteenth century the logician Petrus
Ramus "suggested bringing *inventio* and *dispositio* under dialectics,
leaving to rhetoric only the art of *elocutio*."[33] It was inevitable that
metaphor would take command of that diminished category. Genette has an interest in displacing metaphor from any privileged role.
The essential figurativeness in any language, he maintains, "should
not be *reduced* to metaphor."[34] He has Proust especially in mind. In
Proust, he says, metaphor finds "son appui et sa motivation dans
une métonymie." Proust rarely makes metaphors by transferring a
word from its proper place to another—which is metaphor according to classical rhetoric. The constituents of his metaphors are normally "plus objectif et plus sûr," that is, "les choses voisines et les
mots liés." In Proust, involuntary memory does much of the work
of metaphor. Metaphor is in art what reminiscence is in life, "rapprochement de deux sensations par le 'miracle d'une analogie.'"
Genette argues that this "rapprochement" is "pure de toute métonymie," not metaphor.[35] But it is awkward that Proust evidently
treats metaphor and analogy as synonyms.

Proust offers Genette an immediate if problematic text. He
quotes this passage from *Le Temps retrouvé:*

> On peut faire se succéder indéfiniment dans une description
> les objets qui figuraient dans le lieu décrit, la vérité ne com-
> mencera qu'au moment où l'écrivain prendra deux objets dif-
> férents, posera leur rapport, analogue dans le monde de l'art à
> celui qu'est le rapport unique de la loi causale dans le monde
> de la science, et les enfermera dans les anneaux nécessaires d'un
> beau style; meme, ainsi que la vie, quand, en rapprochant une

qualité commune à deux sensations, il dégagera leur essence
commune en les réunissant l'une et l'autre pour les soustraire
aux contingences du temps, dans une metaphore.[36]

([The writer] can describe a scene by describing one after
another the innumerable objects which at a given moment
were present at a particular place, but truth will be attained
by him only when he takes two different objects, states the
connection between them—a connection analogous in the
world of art to the unique connection which in the world of
science is provided by the law of causality—and encloses
them in the necessary links of a well-wrought style; truth—
and life too—can be attained by us only when, by comparing a quality common to two sensations, we succeed in
extracting their common essence and in reuniting them to
each other, liberated from the contingencies of time, in a
metaphor.)[37]

But a metaphor does not compare a quality common to two
sensations: a simile does that. In a metaphor, the relation between
tenor and vehicle is much more daring than a comparison; it has
nothing in common with the law of causality in science. Genette
concentrates on Proust's claim that he can find "the common
essence" of his two chosen objects and therefore liberate them
from the contingencies of time "in a metaphor." He says:

Thus, between its conscious intentions and its real execution,
Proust's writing falls prey to a singular reversal: having set out
to locate essences, it ends up constituting, or reconstituting,
mirages; intended to reach, through the substantial depth of
the text, the profound substance of things, it culminates in an

effect of phantasmagoric superposition in which the depths cancel each other out, and the substances devour one another. It certainly goes beyond the "superficial" level of a description of appearances, but it does not reach that of a higher realism (the realism of essences), since on the contrary it discovers a level of the real in which reality, by virtue of its plenitude, annihilates *itself*.[38]

The trouble is—or the scandal—that Proust plans to apprehend essences while destroying existences: to exempt himself from time, in fact, by imagining how it would feel to be free of it. He thinks he can do this by abandoning the senses and cultivating only his imagination, metaphor or analogy. His concept of analogy is not the same as Aristotle's proportional metaphor: as A is to B, so C is to D. As Paul Ricoeur says, in metaphor "no appeal is made to the conscious logic of reasoning by analogy."[39] Ricoeur again: "Perception of incompatibility is essential to the interpretation of the message in the case of metaphor."[40] Proust's soul should have trembled before writing that "metaphor alone can give style a sort of eternity."[41] In a different context one would say that Proust committed the heresy of angelism: you can't make a raid on the absolute by ignoring contingencies. Genette justly says that "metaphor, then, like reminiscence, would seem to be merely an indispensable expedient."[42] Nothing is to be gained by claiming that metaphor provides access to eternity: the grace of time is enough. In 1699 Bernard Lamy offered what is still one of the best defenses of metaphor: that it makes all things sensory, gratifying to one's senses. "C'est pourquoi les Poëtes dont le but principal est de plaire, n'employent que ces dernieres expressions: Et c'est pour cette meme raison que les Metaphores qui rendent toutes choses sensibles,

comme nous avons vü, font si frequentes dans leur stile."[43] The
vehicle of a metaphor is rarely an abstraction. Imagine what it
would be if everything in the world were available to one's senses,
the freedom of it.

The sensory capacity of metaphors made it possible, at least
since Aristotle's emphasis on metaphor and resemblance, to bring
into force the whole world of correspondences. As Roberto Calasso noted in his meditation on Baudelaire:

> For centuries, since the first success of Horapollo's *Hieroglyph-*
> *ica,* one may say that European culture was divided between
> the poles of substitution (perceivable in the stubborn deter-
> mination to decipher) and of analogy (perceivable in the
> search for correspondences, and hence for a symbolic chain
> that made it possible, by way of resemblance, to move from
> image to image, without ever abandoning the cosmic play of
> figures).[44]

But the play from image to image is not made by a causal law, as
in logic.

Genette does not propose to undermine metaphor or deny its
capacities. He just wants to ensure that it is treated as one figure
among many. His reduction of metaphor to metonymy, in several
passages of Proust, like Michael Riffaterre's similar reduction of
metaphor in Ponge's "L'Ardoise," is strategic: both critics imply
that the same reduction could be found elsewhere.[45] Genette is obviously pleased when he can show an episode in Proust in which
"la métaphore est ici, apparemment, pure de toute métonymie."[46]
Especially in "Métonymie chez Proust," he is sensitive to "la con-
tagion métonymique" and to its importance "dans l'expérience de
la mémoire involontaire." He ends that essay resoundingly: "Ici

donc, ici seulement—par la métaphore, mais *dans* la métonymie—
ici commence le Recit."[47]

Paul de Man was even bolder: he wanted to displace metaphor by
setting up a rival force. His chosen figure for that purpose was
prosopopeia. In 1821 Pierre Fontanier said that it consisted "in
staging, as it were, absent, dead, supernatural or even inanimate
beings."[48] De Man called it "the fiction of the voice-from-beyond-
the-grave."[49] In other words, it is the trope of apostrophe, of
address by which an absent or nonexistent entity is summoned to
appear. In an essay on Riffaterre, de Man refers to prosopopeia as
"the very figure of the reader and of reading," "the central trope
of the poetic corpus," and later as "the master trope of poetic discourse."[50] In the same essay he extends its range: "Now it is certainly beyond question that the figure of address is recurrent in
lyric poetry, to the point of constituting the generic definition of,
at the very least, the ode (which can, in its turn, be seen as paradig-
matic for poetry in general)."[51] As a test case, de Man then reads a
poem to which Riffaterre has given close attention, Hugo's "Ecrit
sur la vitre d'une fenêtre flamande." Instead of treating it as a descriptive poem, he calls it "a prosopopeia, a giving face to two entities, 'l'heure' and 'l'esprit,' which are most certainly deprived of
any literal face." Here is the poem:

> J'aime le carillon dans tes cités antiques,
> Ö vieux pays gardien de tes moeurs domestiques,
> Noble Flandre, où le Nord se réchauffe engourdi
> Au soleil de Castille et s'accouple au Midi!
> Le carillon, c'est l'heure inattendue et folle,
> Que l'oeil croit voir, vêtue en danseuse espagnole,

Apparaître soudain par le trou vif et clair
Que ferait en s'ouvrant une porte de l'air.
Elle vient, secouant sur les toits léthargiques
Son tablier d'argent plein de notes magiques,
Réveillant sans pitié les dormeurs ennuyeux,
Sautant à petits pas comme un oiseau joyeux,
Vibrant, ainsi qu'un dard qui tremble dans la cible;
Par un frêle escalier de cristal invisible,
Effarée et dansante, elle descend des cieux;
Et l'esprit, ce veilleur fait d'oreilles et d'yeux,
Tandis qu'elle va, vient, monte et descend encore,
Entend de marche en marche errer son pied sonore![52]

Terese Lyons's prose translation, slightly modified, reads:

I love the carillon of your ancient towns, O old land, keeper
of your domestic customs. O noble Flanders, where the be-
numbed North warms itself in the sun of Castile and mates
with the South! The carillon is the unexpected and mad hour
that the eye thinks it sees, dressed as a Spanish dancer, appear-
ing suddenly through the keen, bright hole made by a door of
air as it opens. She comes, shaking over the lethargic rooftops
her silver apron, full of magical notes, pitilessly waking the
bored sleepers, taking little jumps, like a merry bird, quiver-
ing like a spear trembling in its target. By a fragile stairway of
invisible crystal, alarmed and dancing, she descends from the
heavens. And as she goes and comes and climbs up and down
again, the mind, that watchman made of ears and eyes, hears
her resonant foot wandering from step to step.[53]

Riffaterre reads it, to begin with, as a descriptive poem about
the carillon Hugo heard in Mons, or he pretends to read it that

way. By the time he has finished, he has concluded that although "the ideal model for the [poetic] system as a whole is indeed a signified [that is, the carillon in Mons], everything happens as if the signified existed in our minds only as groups of signifiers or as ready-made sequences." To be more specific: "Literary description of reality only gives the appearance of referring to things and signifieds. In point of fact, poetic representation is founded on a reference to signifiers."[54] This could be taken to mean that poems, unlike novels, don't really refer to things in the world. Riffaterre maintains that a poem is a system of signifiers activated by a matrix that is already culturally inscribed in a reader's mind, if she is a competent reader of signs.

De Man goes further, taking his bearings from the apostrophe, "Ö vieux pays." By the end of the poem, he says, "it is possible to identify without fail the *je* and the *tu* of the first line as being time and mind," or rather mind and time. The main generative force that produces the poem, we infer from de Man, is a dance of clichés and conventions, the expansion of the matrix that functions in a purely verbal and not a referential way:

> For the singularity of "Ecrit sur la vitre d'une fenêtre flamande" does not primarily consist of the surprising details; these 'descriptions' can only occur because a consciousness or a mind ("l'esprit") is figurally said to relate to another abstraction (time) as male relates to female in a copulating couple (line 5). The matrix, in other words, is not "carillon" but "j'aime le carillon," and this matrix is not a "donnée sémantique" but is itself already a figure: it is not supposed to describe some peculiar sexual perversion, such as chronophilia, since the persons involved in this affair are persons only by dint of linguistic figuration.[55]

This emphasis on figurality allows de Man to take Hugo's poem as "not the mimesis of a signifier but of a specific figure, prosopopeia." But he has something more in mind:

> This text, like all texts, has to adhere to the program of these problematics, regardless of the philosophical knowledge or skill of its author. It accomplishes the trick by arbitrarily linking the mind to the semiotic relationship that connects the bells to the temporal motion they signify. The senses become the signs of the mind as the sound of the bells is the sign of time, because time and mind are linked, in the figure, as in the embrace of a couple. This declaration ("j'aime le carillon" or *l'esprit aime le temps*) is then acted out, in the erotic mode of 'mere' sense perception, in the allegory of cognition that follows, a seduction scene that culminates in the extraordinary line, the prosopopeia of prosopopeia: *Et l'esprit, ce veilleur fait d'oreilles et d'yeux.*

This meditation allows de Man to complete his rhetoric of prosopopeia: the privileged figure may be "the master trope of poetic discourse," but it is not allowed to have a normative character. Just as Genette and Riffaterre persist in reducing metaphor to metonymy, so de Man reduces prosopopeia to a shadow. Commenting on the extraordinary line from Hugo's poem, de Man says:

> This bizarre waking monster, made of eyes and ears as mud is made of earth and water, is so eminently visible that any attentive reader will have to respond to it. It is the visual shape of something that has no sensory evidence: a hallucination. As any reader of Hugo or, for that matter, anyone who ever wondered about the *legs* of a table or, like Wordsworth, about

the *faces* or the *backs* of mountains, knows, prosopopeia is hallucinatory. To make the invisible visible is uncanny.[56]

The last word, indicating an inevitable *aporia,* is ready:

> How then is one to decide on the distinction between hallu-
> cination and perception since, in hallucination, the difference
> between *I see* and *I think that I see* has been one-sidedly resolved
> in the direction of apperception? Consciousness has become
> consciousness only of itself. In that sense, any consciousness,
> including perception, is hallucinatory: one never "has" a hal-
> lucination the way one has a sore foot from kicking the pro-
> verbial stone. Just as the hypothesis of dreaming undoes the
> certainty of sleep, the hypothesis, or the figure, of hallucina-
> tion undoes sense certainty. This means, in linguistic terms,
> that it is impossible to say whether prosopopeia is plausible
> because of the empirical existence of dreams and hallucinations
> or whether one believes that such things as dreams and hallu-
> cinations exist because language permits the figure of proso-
> popeia. The question "Was it a vision or a waking dream?" is
> destined to remain unanswered. Prosopopeia undoes the dis-
> tinction between reference and signification on which all
> semiotic systems, including Riffaterre's, depend.[57]

So de Man reaches, not for the first time, the point at which his
version of deconstruction merges with the history of skepticism
and must submit to the same interrogations. I have nothing to add
to Stanley Cavell's list of those. But I demur at de Man's assertion
that prosopopeia is always hallucinatory. We are not troubled by
the *leg* of a table or the *back* of a mountain if we recall that the first
generation of metaphors was drawn from the parts of the human

body: the *hair* of the dog, the *head* of the table, the *eye* of the storm, the *mouth* of the river, the *lip* of the jug, the *heart* of the matter, the *side* of a mountain, a *chest* of drawers, the *arm* of the chair, the *hands* of God, the *foot* of the bed, the *heel* of the hunt.

I have no strong objection to de Man's advocacy of prosopopeia except to say that someone must put a face on the absent one and there's little point in claiming that the someone is only such "by dint of linguistic figuration." Of course Hamlet is someone only by such dint, but we experience the play by putting this notion in brackets and attending to the semblances as if they were, for the time being, real. We do the same when we come upon a metaphor: we practice the aesthetic of "as if." We are not on oath. But the hard problem about prosopopoeia, if it is supposed to displace metaphor, is that not all poems or novels are in the vocative case. Some are. When I read Hardy's "The Voice"—"Woman much missed, how you call to me, call to me"—I am aware that I am reading a lyric and that the speaker's stance is one of prosopopoeia, but I can't avoid responding to the poem also as an adventure among the elected rhyming words—in the first stanza, "call," "call," and nearly inevitably, "all"; in the second, "you," "view," "drew," "knew," "blue," the "you" repeated three times; in the third, more questionably, "breeze," "listlessness," and "wistlessness"; and in the fourth and last, where the vowel in "call" from the first stanza is recalled with variations:

> Thus I; faltering forward,
> Leaves around me falling,
> Wind oozing thin through the thorn from norward,
> And the woman calling.[58]

What we respond to is Hardy's pain in trying to invoke her, to call her voice into being, and his failing, though he claims he succeeds. In the first line and the last he imagines that the dead woman is calling to him, rather than that he is calling to her, though he is indeed calling to her. And why does he call her, in the last line, "the woman"? I have to note, for what it's worth, that the poem is poor in metaphors, except for "Wind oozing thin." There are many things to pay attention to, in addition to prosopopeia. Besides, prosopopeia can either succeed or fail, contrary to de Man who says that it always fails by definition.

Some writers—I mean poets, novelists, dramatists—would get rid of metaphor if they could. Beckett, for one, on receipt of a parcel of metaphors, would inscribe on it: "Return to sender. Thanks a lot, but no thanks." But he can't. Metaphors and personifications keep breaking in, as in *Words and Music* when Words says:

> Some moments later, however, such are the powers of recuperation at this age, the head is drawn back to a distance of two or three feet, the eyes widen to a stare and begin to feast again. . . . What then is seen would have been better seen in the light of day, that is incontestable. But how often has it not, in recent months, how often, at all hours, under all angles, in cloud and shine, been seen, I mean. And there is, is there not, in that clarity of silver . . . that clarity of silver . . . is there not . . . my Lord . . . Now and then the rye, swayed by a light wind, casts and withdraws its shadow.[59]

The eyes "begin to feast again." More metaphor than personification, I think. "The rye, swayed by a light wind, casts and withdraws its shadow." Personification.

The Motive for Metaphor

the magnetic attraction of the similar
—Jacques Derrida

*t*he strongest motive for metaphor known to me is conveyed by Quintilian in a glowing passage:

> [Metaphor] is both a gift which Nature herself confers on us, and which is therefore used even by uneducated persons and unconsciously, and at the same time so attractive and elegant that it shines by its own light however splendid its context. So long as it is correctly employed, it cannot be vulgar or mean or unpleasing. It also adds to the resources of language by exchanges or borrowings to supply its deficiencies, and (hardest task of all) it ensures that nothing goes without a name (praestat ne ulli rei nomen deesse videatur) (8.6.5).

"It ensures that nothing goes without a name": a beautiful, caring motive.

Sometimes it can be achieved without much ado: a word is taken out of its proper setting and placed elsewhere for some good purpose. Yeats's poem "In Memory of Eva Gore-Booth and Con Markiewicz" speaks of the sisters and of their great house, Lissadell:

> Many a time I think to seek
> One or the other out and speak
> Of that old Georgian mansion, mix
> Pictures of the mind, recall
> That gable and the talk of youth,
> Two girls in silk kimonos, both
> Beautiful, one a gazelle.[1]

It's not a simile. Yeats is not saying that the girl "is like a gazelle" in some one respect, though that would be much. The OED says that "the gazelle is especially noted for the grace of its movements and the softness of its eyes." In the metaphor, the girl's nature goes over into the nature of a gazelle as if both came from one luminous source. That is what naming comes to: it is not a matter of glancing at an attribute here or there but of acknowledging a complete nature and giving it its destined name. The rhyming of "Lissadell" and "gazelle" may have suggested the animal to Yeats. It hardly matters. The invoking of the two girls, followed by the alliterative enjambement—"both / Beautiful"—makes a strong setting for "one a gazelle."

Quintilian's motive can't always be fulfilled. There is no reason to assume that there are words for everything, though we proceed as if there were. The source of metaphor is the liberty of the mind among such words as there are. In metaphors, we cry out to change the world by giving things their proper names—which they have lacked—but often we fail to get the names right. Still, we press hard upon the words we choose, often to little avail. Hans Blumenberg has maintained that "the axiom of all rhetoric is the principle of insufficient reason (*principium rationis insufficientis*)":

> It is a correlate of the anthropology of a creature who is deficient in essential respects. If man's world accorded with the optimism of the metaphysics of Leibniz, who thought that he could assign a sufficient reason even for the fact that anything exists at all, rather than nothing (*"cur aliquid potius quam nihil"*), then there would be no rhetoric, because there would be neither the need nor the possibility of using it effectively.[2]

Rhetoric, it appears, is a glorious failure, and the cry of metaphor is doomed: we can't, after all, change the world by finding names for things. We can make worldlings feel ashamed of themselves, if they are capable of feeling ashamed when they see their cruel idiology disgraced, shown up for the falsity it propounds. That, I suppose, is something.

But metaphor is so resourceful, within that dire restriction, that the force of it expands in several directions. Allegory is its narrative form—"Métaphore prolongée et continue," as Fontanier calls it—the extension of metaphor that takes personification into its orbit: the particles of metaphor take on the dramatic attributes of character, story, scene, and moral charge.[3] Catachresis is the figure of its abuse. In English, it is indistinguishable from the conceit, when an image is driven beyond itself or at least beyond the decorous forms of itself, regardless of manners and good taste. Fontanier is our authority on this, especially when he describes catachreses of metonymy, of synecdoche, and (most elaborately) of metaphor.[4] None of these is an aberration: to speak of "forced metaphor" is not to degrade its manifestations. Indeed, Fontanier goes so far as to proclaim them as "sans doute, justes et naturelles."[5] But, as Paul de Man says: "Something monstrous lurks in the most innocent of catachreses: when one speaks of the legs of the table or the face of the mountain, catachresis is already turning into prosopopeia, and one begins to perceive a world of potential ghosts and monsters."[6] Or at least of shadowy, conjured presences, like Frost's "enormous Glacier," in "Directive," "That braced his feet against the Arctic Pole."[7]

Wallace Stevens's poem "The Motive for Metaphor" reads:

> You like it under the trees in autumn,
> Because everything is half dead.
> The wind moves like a cripple among the leaves
> And repeats words without meaning.
>
> In the same way, you were happy in spring,
> With the half colors of quarter-things,
> The slightly brighter sky, the melting clouds,
> The single bird, the obscure moon—
>
> The obscure moon lighting an obscure world
> Of things that would never be quite expressed,
> Where you yourself were never quite yourself
> And did not want nor have to be,
>
> Desiring the exhilarations of changes:
> The motive for metaphor, shrinking from
> The weight of primary noon,
> The A B C of being,

> The ruddy temper, the hammer
> Of red and blue, the hard sound—
> Steel against intimation—the sharp flash,
> The vital, arrogant, fatal, dominant X.[8]

The accredited interpretation—Northrop Frye's—goes somewhat like this. What Stevens variously calls "the weight of primary noon, the A B C of being," and the "dominant X" is "the objective world, the world set over against us." His aim is "to show you a world completely absorbed and possessed by the human mind": "The motive for metaphor, according to Wallace Stevens, is a desire to associate, and finally to identify, the human mind with what goes on outside it, because the only genuine joy you can have is in those rare moments when you feel that although we may know in part, as Paul says (1 Cor. 13:9), we are also a part of what we know."[9] I have seen another interpretation, sufficiently different to be worth reciting, in which John Crowe Ransom, thinking of Hegel and the "Concrete Universal," finds Stevens's poem much to the point. He describes the "Universal" in this way:

> A Universal in Hegel's favorite sense is any idea in the mind which proposes a little universe, or organized working combination of parts, where there is a whole and single effect to be produced, and the heterogeneous parts must perform their several duties faithfully in order to bring it about. Thus the formula of a chemical reaction; the recipe of a dish; the blueprint of a machine; or even, to the extent in which it is practicable, Newman's "idea of a university." It becomes a Concrete Universal when it has been materialized and is actually working. The Universal is likely to be stubborn because it sets the terms upon which the whole transaction proceeds. Indeed, it

may be just as recalcitrant as "the world set over against us," except that it depends upon the mind that respects it; it is not external to that.

Having quoted Stevens's poem entire, Ransom paraphrases it for his occasion:

> That is to say, I think, something like the following. "You like metaphor in the autumn, because you cannot express yourself, except to say that the wind cannot express itself either. You like it in the spring, because instead of trying to express what you feel then, you can speak of how the obscure moon lights an obscure world. You like it because it is exhilarating, and alternative to the dreary searching of your own mind for the meaning of your state. (There must be many a moral Universal seeking its poetry though it is no better than a moral feeling; so much of the moral life turns on feeling, and on half-successful reflection, and can scarcely ever be satisfied except with a poetic expression or its homely equivalent.) The moral Universal is intolerably harsh and simple, when you phrase it, not equal to what you want it to mean, and in fact it is the 'vital, arrogant, fatal, dominant X'; it is inexpressive, like the sign of an unknown quantity."[10]

It is not necessary to make peace or war between these readers, beyond saying that Frye takes the "X" to be the objective world set over against us and Ransom takes it to be one of our own moral universals, resolutely harsh until it finds itself agreeably fulfilled in the concrete detail of a natural or a human world. Metaphor is the prime means of the satisfaction that Frye envisages, and perhaps Ransom would find it so too, though he does not mention it.

Metaphor is a figure of speech, an act of the mind largely independent of "the world set over against us." But only largely, because in literature the mind acts upon a particular language and lives within its inventive constraints. Writers have to say to themselves, "my nature is subdued / to what it works in, like the dyer's hand."[11] We usually think of metaphors as additions to the world; they add perceptions that were not there before. But if the motive for metaphor, according to Stevens, is to defeat or evade the force of the world, it must resort to the imaginative capacity of the mind and exert its freedom to do just that—or at worst to try. Stevens says, in one of his notes on poetry, that "reality is a cliché from which we escape by metaphor," and lest we miss the point, he adds that "it is only *au pays de la métaphore qu'on est poète*." In the same notebook he concedes that if you want to change real objects "without the aid of metaphor," you could do so "by feeling, style etc." He also says that "Metaphor creates a new reality from which the original appears to be unreal."[12]

Stevens was not a trained philosopher, but his desires were philosophic. Mostly, he hoped against hope that idealism would turn out to be true: that consciousness would be found to account for the whole of one's experience. In most of his moods he was a Hegelian, in the spirit of Hegel's introduction to his lectures on aesthetics, published posthumously:

> The universal need for art . . . is man's rational need to lift the
> inner and outer world into his spiritual consciousness as an
> object in which he recognizes again his own self. The need
> for this spiritual freedom he satisfies, on the one hand, within
> by making what is within him explicit to himself, but corre-
> spondingly by giving outward reality to this his explicit self;

and thus in this duplication of himself by bringing what is in him into sight and knowledge for himself and others. This is the free rationality of man in which all acting and knowing, as well as art too, have their basis and necessary origin.[13]

So Stevens wrote of Adam:

> We knew one parent must have been divine,
> Adam of beau regard, from fat Elysia,
> Whose mind malformed this morning metaphor,
>
> While all the leaves leaked gold. His mind made morning,
> As he slept. He woke in a metaphor: this was
> A metamorphosis of paradise.[14]

More generally, as in "Description without Place":

> It is possible that to seem—it is to be,
> As the sun is something seeming and it is.
>
> The sun is an example. What it seems
> It is and in such seeming all things are.[15]

Stevens's aim was, as in a Paterian irony directed at Matthew Arnold, to see the object as in itself it really seems to be, and to be content with that. But in certain moods he faced the obstacles to that desire. In "Notes toward a Supreme Fiction" he wrote:

> From this the poem springs: that we live in a place
> That is not our own and, much more, not ourselves
> And hard it is in spite of blazoned days.[16]

"Much more" is much worse. That the world should be ourselves is a wild hope unless one is a convinced idealist, but Stevens had moods so diverse that we find him believing nearly anything. Sometimes he longed for simplicity, the convergence of word and thing, the truth of things as the man in the street takes it to be. In "An Ordinary Evening in New Haven" he wrote:

> We seek
> The poem of pure reality, untouched
> By trope or deviation, straight to the word,
> Straight to the transfixing object, to the object
> At the exactest point at which it is itself,
> Transfixing by being purely what it is,
> A view of New Haven, say, through the certain eye,
>
> The eye made clear of uncertainty, with the sight
> Of simple seeing, without reflection. . . . [17]

But he felt misgiving about planning to see anything "at the exactest point at which it is itself." That way, naturalism lies—fixity, and specious certitude. For the time being, in "The Motive for Metaphor," he can only cry out against the "dominant X." He was not alone in that protest. Ortega y Gasset maintained that the chief motive of art since Baudelaire, Mallarmé, and Debussy has been to reject the conventional privilege ascribed to external things, objects, and faces, and to cultivate entirely formal, aesthetic inventions. I assume he had modern abstract or nonfigurative paintings in view, and knew that these had their own authority, however occult. That is why Stevens was pleased to find Charles Mauron saying, in his *Aesthetics and Psychology* (1935), that "the artist transforms us, willy-nilly, into epicures."[18] He was also pleased to find, in Simone Weil's *La Pesanteur et la grâce,* a chapter on "decreation." Stevens commented: "She says that decreation is making [something] pass from the created to the uncreated, but that destruction is making [something] pass from the created to nothingness. Modern reality is a reality of decreation."[19] He was pleased too to find Picasso saying that a picture is a horde of destructions, if only because it allowed Stevens to say that "a poem is a horde of destructions."[20] Metaphor, according to Ortega, has been the main device in an artist's rejection of external things. "Metaphor alone furnishes an escape." Its efficacy verges on magic. Between real things, it "lets emerge imaginary reefs, a crop of floating islands." Metaphor "disposes of an object by having it masquerade as something else."[21] We ascribe to Nietzsche but not only to him the desire to be elsewhere, which is a variant of the desire to be different.[22] In certain moods the horror of a word is the meaning it defends against all comers, so metaphor is the device by which one undermines that defense. In Stevens's "Someone Puts a Pineapple Together" the someone contemplates "A wholly artificial nature, in which / The profusion of metaphor has been increased." If you put a pineapple together and see metaphors becoming more profuse, you release yourself from psychological determinations; you become a performative gesture and are happy to find yourself in that state. But then a scruple may assert itself:

> He must say nothing of the fruit that is
> Not true, nor think it, less. He must defy
> The metaphor that murders metaphor.[23]

Presumably a bad metaphor murders a good one: bad in the sense of telling lies, ignoring the truths that can't honorably be ignored.

Even among Stevens's various practices, the structure of "The Motive for Metaphor" is peculiar. The first stanza coincides with two simple, parallel sentences. A third sentence is stretched out over the remainder of the poem, not because the syntax becomes complex—it doesn't—but because one phrase is instructed to produce another by association, and that one to bring forward yet another by a similar device. The practice is common in Stevens, where a particular clause tends not to reach conclusion but to keep the discourse going by stirring a further association, an echo or a repetition—"Disguised pronunciamento, summary, / Autumn's compendium. . . ." His sentences tend not to be decisive, he is reluctant to concede that a poem has to end. We sometimes wonder if he is a man without will. Does he take pleasure in withholding himself, as if keeping a secret? If we go from reading Frost, say, who is always willful, to Stevens, who seems to write poems by letting phrases write themselves. We recall that in "The Creations of Sound" he said that "there are words / Better without an author, without a poet, / Or having a separate author, a different poet, / An accretion from ourselves, intelligent / Beyond intelligence, an artificial man / At a distance, a secondary expositor. . . ."[24] In "The Motive for Metaphor" the repetition of "the obscure moon" is labored, the momentum has to be started up again, until the appositive colon after "changes" is reached and the long sentence continues, specifying the nature of the desire. Even when Stevens designates something, the thing he designates is rarely allowed to speak for itself or to bring the sentence to an end; he must apply his commodious adjectives to every noun. It would be fair to say of Stevens's poems what Hazlitt said of Wordsworth's *The Excursion,* that "an intense intellectual egotism swallows up everything": "There is, in fact, in Mr. Wordsworth's mind (if we may hazard the conjecture) a repugnance to admit anything that tells for itself, without the interpretation of the poet—a fastidious antipathy to immediate effect—a systematic unwillingness to share the poem with his subject."[25] Stevens seems reluctant to end a sentence, even when he comes to a noun or a verb that could well end it; he always sees a further possibility, yet another variation on the theme, a new way of putting it. The process is more metonymy than metaphor: one word, then another, then another, each of them laid down one after its fellow in a congenially suggestive place. They are not meant to disturb one another. But the trouble with this device is that it often makes it impossible to decide whether the several phrases have equal value, or whether they merely happen to lie contiguously in Stevens's mind. The procedure might be called additive, except that Stevens is not much interested in bringing the additions up to a definition, a sum of attributions. It might be called linear if a line were allowed, as it is allowed in many paintings by Klee, to extend itself apparently at will. So it is a shock to find "The Motive for Metaphor" driving to an end when four adjectives hit a wall in "X."

"You like it": I take this as a variant of "one likes metaphor," one being anyone who appreciates metaphor when the weather of things is dull. But other readings are possible: that the "you" is someone, not necessarily Stevens, who wants life to be mobile, changeable without notice, and looks to metaphor to bring these felicities about; or that the "you" is one of Stevens's earlier selves whom he is now determined to chastise. This last is Helen Vendler's interpretation, and she gives it with characteristic verve. She thinks "The Motive of Metaphor" a "very brutal poem," propelled by "self-loathing" and "self-contempt." The speaking voice "detests those exhilarations of changes which are the motive for metaphor." She thinks the poem welcomes "the exhilaration of a new sort of self-knowledge, a change into the changelessness of a final, permanent self." This may entail "the last possible phase, the fatal phase, and therefore the end of poetry."[26] I would assent to this interpretation except that I don't recall any occasion on which Stevens demanded a final, changeless self for himself or spent much energy trying to bring it about. I think it was from Stevens I derived my affection for aspects, the boy turning a globe slowly in his hands, waiting for the next gift.

The change to the past tense in the second stanza—"you were happy in spring"—gives the "you" a certain density, almost historical, in passing from autumn to spring. The choice remains between virtually taking "you" to mean "I" or taking it to mean someone else. So the stance of the poem could be either sympathetic, to the degree of willed identity with the "you," or diagnostic, standing in judgment upon "you," as Helen Vendler would have it. But the later stanzas of the poem seem to merge the "you" with an unstated "I," the "I" being the voice of the anonymous speaker of the poem. Autumn and spring are named, but not summer which has its felicities elsewhere and often in Stevens's poems. Stevens told Charles Tomlinson that when he wrote the poem "Credences of Summer," "my feeling for the necessity of a final accord with reality was at its strongest: reality was the summer of the title of the book in which the poem appeared."[27] Metaphor is not needed when summer is lavish—

> Trace the gold sun about the whitened sky
> Without evasion by a single metaphor.[28]

—an impossible task, such that only the desire for it survives. In "Credences of Summer" Stevens evokes "the first autumnal inhalations": presumably these breathings take metaphors—or the im-

ages of metaphors—into the speaker's lungs for life. The wind
refutes Shelley's "Ode to the West Wind" by disclaiming its mes-
sages: "words without meaning." Stevens's poem anticipates a
greater poem, "The Course of a Particular," in which he silences
Shelley's ode again.

"In the same way, you were happy in spring." The first phrase
is blunt, in the absence of reasons why the two ways should be the
same. In "Credences of Summer" Stevens speaks of "spring's in-
furiations" as if the season were mad to achieve its summer. Here
it is content with the beginnings of change—"The slightly brighter
sky, the melting clouds." Patient, spring is willing to wait for
changes—which is the best that can be said for the repetition that
follows: "the obscure moon— / The obscure moon lighting an
obscure world / Of things that would never be quite expressed."
The verbal whispering continues by repeating "yourself" and coming to rest, but not to conclusion, with "desiring the exhilarations
of changes." "It Must Change" is one of the sectional insistences
of "Notes toward a Supreme Fiction." It need not be any particular change; it is change for the sake of change, as if the condition
most to be feared were boredom or the fixity of things. Another
of the insistences of "Notes toward a Supreme Fiction" is that "It
Must Give Pleasure," and the main pleasure seems to be the exhilarations of changes, the reluctance to see anything remain settled
in itself. The particular motive for metaphor is given in a clause—
"shrinking from / The weight of primary noon."

Shrinking is a common gesture in Stevens's work: he shrinks
from anything too well established. Objects in their settled forms
are put under scrutiny. Majestic conceptions are driven out of themselves at whatever cost, as in "Esthétique du Mal":

> This is a part of the sublime
> From which we shrink. And yet, except for us,
> The total past felt nothing when destroyed.[29]

In "Thinking of a Relation between the Images of Metaphors," the poor fish, the bass, fearful of Indian fishermen "keep looking ahead, upstream, in one / Direction, shrinking from the spit and splash / Of waterish spears."[30] In "Effects of Analogy" Stevens says: "A poet writes of twilight because he shrinks from noon-day."[31] In "The Figure of the Youth as Virile Poet" he says: "If a man's nerves shrink from loud sounds, they are quite likely to shrink from strong colors and he will be found preferring a drizzle in Venice to a hard rain in Hartford."[32] The best that can be said for shrinking is that it may enable you, under pressure, to practice a defensive economy, as in "Description without Place"—

> There might be, too, a change immenser than
> A poet's metaphors in which being would
>
> Come true, a point in the fire of music where
> Dazzle yields to a clarity and we observe,
>
> And observing is completing and we are content,
> In a world that shrinks to an immediate whole,
>
> That we do not need to understand, complete
> Without secret arrangements of it in the mind.[33]

But metaphor itself does not shrink. It is what you do after shrinking: you escape by turning to antinomian values, aesthetic values of form and style. If I were reading "The Motive for Metaphor" aloud or to myself, I would give the line "The motive for metaphor, shrinking from" four nearly equal accents, the one on "from" sustaining the eight specifications that lead to "X." These eight are versions of fixity, each of them presumably repellent, mighty nuisances that can't be easily dissolved. "Steel against intimation" is the hardest of them.

The adjectives that bring the last line of "The Motive for Metaphor" to an end come from different families: "vital," the principle or force essential to organic life, here irrefutable; "arrogant," as if the "X" were someone, alert to his invincible character; "fatal," as if destined, inevitable; "dominant," commanding, but it may come from music, where it means the fifth note of the scale of any key, of special importance to the harmonies of that key. Finally, "X," an unknown quantity, produced several times in Stevens's poems with secretive intent, though on one occasion, in "The Creations of Sound," he refers to "X" as "an obstruction, a man / Too exactly himself," and the man seems to be T. S. Eliot. A man too exactly himself is open to the deconstructive attention of metaphor.

Stevens associated metaphor with several other words that he was happy to keep in its vicinity: metamorphosis, likeness, resemblance, analogy. He often used these interchangeably, but he was careful to distinguish them from identity and imitation. His cardinal word was resemblance: he invoked it as if it were beyond question. In "Three Academic Pieces" he referred to "one of the significant components of the structure of reality—that is to say, the resemblance between things." But his sense of resemblance was latitudinarian: "in some sense, all things resemble each other." As if to prove this grand principle, he wrote:

Take, for example, a beach extending as far as the eye can reach, bordered, on the one hand, by trees and, on the other, by the sea. The sky is cloudless and the sun is red. In what sense do the objects in this scene resemble each other? There is enough green in the sea to relate it to the palms. There is enough of the sky reflected in the water to create a resemblance, in some sense, between them. The sand is yellow between the green and the blue. In short, the light alone creates a unity not only in the recedings of distance, where differences become invisible, but also in the contacts of closer sight. . . . So, too, sufficiently generalized, each man resembles all other men, each woman resembles all other women, this year resembles last year.[34]

And so on. In no time, Stevens is ready to say that "in metaphor, the resemblance may be, first, between two or more parts of reality; second, between something real and something imagined or, what is the same thing, between something imagined and something real as, for example, between music and whatever may be evoked by it; and, third, between two imagined things as when we say that God is good, since the statement involves a resemblance between two concepts, a concept of God and a concept of goodness." Resemblance "in metaphor is an activity of the imagination; and in metaphor the imagination is life." Musing further, Stevens suggests that "perhaps resemblance which seems to be related so closely to the imagination is related even more closely to the intelligence, of which perceptions of resemblance are effortless accelerations."[35]

It may be said that Stevens had Aristotle's authority in deeming resemblance to amount to a critical principle, but there are differences. Aristotle does not hold that anything resembles, in some respect, anything else. In the *Metaphysics* he carefully indicates when two things may be called "like": "Things are called 'like' which have the same attributes in all respects; or more of those attributes the same than different; or whose quality is one. Also that which has a majority or the more important of those attributes of something else in respect of which change is possible (i.e. the contraries) is like that thing."[36] In the *Poetics* (1459a3–8) and the *Rhetoric* (1412a10) he says that making a good metaphor requires an intuitive perception of the similarity in dissimilars: that is the mark of genius. Stevens is never as careful; he sets the bar of similarity so low walking along the beach with his greens and blues and yellows that he makes resemblance an empty principle. Indeed, his confidence in resemblance and similarity is misplaced; it would not survive interrogation, specifically Nelson Goodman's seven strictures in *Problems and Projects* (1972). Goodman shows that similarity is not a quality of things in themselves: "It is relative, variable and culture-dependent." Statements of similarity "are still serviceable in the streets" but not in more exacting places. "Similarity does not explain metaphor or metaphorical truth." Goodman agrees with Max Black that "it would be more illuminating in some of these cases to say that the metaphor creates the similarity than to say that it formulates some similarity antecedently existing."[37] "Similarity cannot be equated with, or measured in terms of, possession of common characteristics." Finally for my purpose, "as it occurs in philosophy, similarity tends under analysis either to vanish entirely or to require for its explanation just what it purports to explain."[38] Stevens does not question the explanatory power of resemblance; he seems to take it as a natural law, one of nature's choice gifts to poets.

But at least once he admits dissimilarity, in Aristotle's terms. In "Three Academic Pieces" he says that "poetry is a satisfying of the desire for resemblance":

> As the mere satisfying of a desire, it is pleasurable. But poetry if it did nothing but satisfy a desire would not rise above the level of many lesser things. Its singularity is that in the act of satisfying the desire for resemblance it touches the sense of reality, it enhances the sense of reality, heightens it, intensifies it. If resemblance is described as a partial similarity between two dissimilar things, it complements and reinforces that which the two dissimilar things have in common.[39]

As an example, Stevens quotes *Ecclesiastes* (12:6): "Or ever the silver cord be loosed, or the golden bowl be broken, or the pitcher be broken at the fountain, or the wheel broken at the cistern" and says, "These images are not the language of reality, they are the symbolic language of metamorphosis, or resemblance, of poetry, but they relate to reality and they intensify our sense of it and they give us the pleasure of 'lentor and solemnity' in respect to the most commonplace objects."[40]

Lentor and *solemnity* are, I think, musical terms, *lentor* meaning "slowness." But Stevens does not mention the most acute quality of a metaphor, that to bring it forward you must force the issue, driving the vehicle to the extreme limit of identity. You must compel attention to the whole vehicle, not just to the qualities on which a strict comparison would thrive. If you take the metaphor seriously, you provoke the resistance of common sense, and commit the audacity of a conceit. No such *frisson* arises with a simile. A simile compares one thing to another, without changing either of the entities compared; it is a tangent that doesn't dislodge the circle it touches. A metaphor incurs resistance from our sense of absurdity and is indifferent to shame.

Stevens's metaphors are often bizarre. One of the poems I have referred to, "Someone Puts a Pineapple Together," is an elaborate and rather strained meditation on subject and object, the several stages in the process of perceiving something, an object on a table, which—the object—turns out to be or to become a pineapple. In the third section, Stevens has a fancy out of *Gulliver's Travels* in which the someone in question climbs up the side of a pineapple—

> The momentary footings of a climb
> Up the pineapple, a table Alp and yet
> An Alp, a purple Southern mountain bisqued
>
> With the molten mixings of related things,
> Cat's taste possibly or possibly Danish lore,
> The small luxuriations that portend
>
> Universal delusions of universal grandeurs,
> The slight incipiencies, of which the form,
> At last, is the pineapple on the table or else
>
> An object the sum of its complications, seen
> And unseen.[41]

"Bisqued": the OED doesn't recognize the word or know any verb the past participle of which is "bisqued." Bisque has a frail existence in the vocabularies of tennis, croquet, and pottery, but the common bisque as a variant of "bisk" means a thick soup made by boiling down birds, especially pigeons, or fish, especially crayfish or lobsters. "The molten mixings of related things" suggests that Stevens has soup in mind. "A purple Southern mountain" is the tenor of the metaphor, "bisqued" and its mixings are the vehicle. The propriety of the metaphor is not in question. Common sense would have advised Stevens to drop the bisque, but Stevens would have answered: "I've fetched it so far, I'll stick with it." It becomes a conceit, though not a becoming one. Not that mountains are unchangeable in Stevens. He has a poem called "The Poem That Took the Place of a Mountain," in which a mountain has to shift itself, allow its cones to be moved, to improve the view. But "bisqued" suggests that Stevens has been looking with some envy at Dali's liquefied watch. Goodman says of a metaphor that it is "an affair between a predicate with a past and an object that yields while protesting."[42] "Bisqued" must have produced a loud, sustained protest, unless the mountain was already accustomed to the mannerist Stevens.

But Stevens's metaphors are rarely as weird as that one. Turning the pages of "An Ordinary Evening in New Haven," I note first this one that is comfortably urbane:

Why, then, inquire
Who has divided the world, what entrepeneur?
No man. The self, the chrysalis of all men

Became divided in the leisure of blue day
And more, in branchings after day. One part
Held fast tenaciously in common earth

And one from central earth to central sky
And in moonlit extensions of them in the mind
Searched out such majesty as it could find.[43]

"Chrysalis": "the state into which the larva of most insects passes before becoming an imago or perfect insect. In this state the insect is inactive and takes no food, and is wrapped in a hard sheath or case" (OED). I'm not sure how much of this account gets into Stevens's metaphor or what "the self" in this case is supposed to mean. Not sure either what the later, decisive stage of "the self" could be that finds itself in "all men" before being divided into two parts, one of them that holds to "common earth," the other one that engages in lunar searchings.

Poem 15 of "An Ordinary Evening in New Haven" has a passage so winning that I am inclined to take it on the run without stopping on any detail, but the metaphorical detail is among its choice blessings:

> The hibernal dark that hung
> In primavera, the shadow of bare rock,
>
> Becomes the rock of autumn, glittering,
> Ponderable source of each imponderable,
> The weight we lift with the finger of a dream,
>
> The heaviness we lighten by light will,
> By the hand of desire, faint, sensitive, the soft
> Touch and trouble of the touch of the actual hand.[44]

Here the metaphorical intention is distributed along the sentence, starting with the fancy contrast of "hibernal" and "primavera." It gathers force in "The weight we lift with the finger of a dream," but the metaphor does not complete itself until desire is accomplished in "the hand of desire" and its adjectival consummation, "faint, sensitive, the soft / Touch and trouble of the touch of the actual hand." It is unfortunate that we have to fend off the vulgar association of "a soft touch"—"a person easily manipulated." "Trouble" comes a little too late to save the day. But the entire sentence, rich in metaphor, is admirably shaped.

The impulse in metaphor to escape from the world, and especially from the importunity of objects, things, and faces, is best fulfilled by putting another form of discourse in place of reference. The strongest such form is prophecy. Shelley said in *A Defence of Poetry* that metaphorical language "marks the before unapprehended relations of things and perpetuates their apprehension until words, which represent them, become, through time, signs for portions or classes of thought, instead of pictures of integral thoughts."[45] The passage from Paul's letter to the Corinthians that Northrop Frye referred to many pages back is much in point. Paul is speaking of charity as "the greatest of these," greater even than "the gift of prophecy." But even as a second-best, prophecy survives: it is one of life's expressive forms. The passage reads: "Charity never faileth: but whether there be prophecies, they shall fail; whether there be tongues, they shall cease; whether there be knowledge, it shall vanish away. For we know in part, and we prophesy in part. But when that which is perfect is come, then that which is in part shall be done away" (1 Cor. 13:8–10).

"To prophesy": to speak as by divine inspiration and therefore to claim access to the future, as Antony says, prophesying over the wounds of Julius Caesar: "A curse shall light upon the limbs of men." More generally, it is to speak without any producible authority, scorning mere designation, to speak by *fiat*. Likewise, metaphor acknowledges no authority. Nothing in the given world authorizes "bisqued"; it has not even been in English until now. For all we know, it may enter the language as a metaphorical nuance, or it may be rejected as a bizarrerie.

But Stevens's normal sense of metaphor is not bizarre. In the note on reality and metaphor from which I've quoted, he says that, some objects being less susceptible to metaphor than others, "the absolute object slightly turned is a metaphor of the object," and that "the whole world is less susceptible to metaphor than a tea-cup is."[46] True, it is harder to keep "the whole world" in mind than to hold a tea cup there, and perhaps that is reason enough, but the image of turning the globe around is just as feasible as that of twisting a cup in its saucer and holding it up to a various light. The turning seems to be the metaphorical point; it was enough even for Hegel, who was charmed by the freedom of it, as if the object, turned freely in the hand, were enough. Even in Stevens's most somber moods, as in "Metaphor as Degeneration," when he has assured himself that "being / Includes death and the imagination," he assembles enough spirit to proclaim a rhetorical question. It is as if he were replying to Max Nordau, in whose *Degeneration* (1892) we find nearly every modern institution trounced as degenerate, science the sole honorable exemption. But Stevens is prepared to ask—

> How, then, is metaphor degeneration,
> When Swatara becomes this undulant river
> And the river becomes the landless, waterless ocean?

—even though he ends with grim recognitions—

> Here the black violets grow down to its banks
> And the memorial mosses hang their green
> Upon it, as it flows ahead.[47]

That "ahead" is hard to bear: if we can put up with it, we can put up with anything.

But it is time to say that "The Motive for Metaphor" presents its experience as a blank failure. Nothing in the poem defeats the final "X." If we bring Hegel's criteria to bear on it, we have to report that the poem fails "to lift the inner and outer world into [man's] spiritual consciousness as an object in which he recognizes again his own self." This accounts for the rage and despair in the poem's final lines; the steely list is a selection of the typical things Stevens can't lift into his spiritual consciousness. He can act with an appearance of freedom—Hegel's favorite word in that part of the lectures—but the things of the palpably external world are too dogged, too heavy, too sullen to be lifted into that place of spirituality. For the moment, metaphor names a desire, a motive, but only a partial achievement at best. Idealists lose in the end. They shouldn't have made such a demand, but it is a noble defeat, if only because they speak up so eloquently for the mind— the mind, "among the creatures that it makes, / The people, those by which it lives and dies."[48] I wish that Stevens had written "those by whom it lives and dies," but he didn't and there it is.

We can't expect from Stevens a definitive statement about metaphor, or indeed about anything. There is always another mood in which he turns the tea cup still farther around and sees it differently. Mostly, he says of metaphor that it entails "the real made more acute by an unreal," as in "The Bouquet,"[49] but he has another mood in which, seeing a bouquet of roses in sunlight, he says of them that they are—

> Too much as they are to be changed by metaphor,
> Too actual, things that in being real
> Make any imaginings of them lesser things.

If Stevens had held to this as a conviction, our reading of him would have had to be entirely different: we would have taken him as a sturdy realist, a poet of the eighteenth century. But one mood displaced its predecessor, like a new paradigm in Thomas Kuhn's history of scientific revolutions:

> Our sense of these things changes and they change,
> Not as in metaphor, but in our sense
> Of them. So sense exceeds all metaphor.

If this little display of another logic is a scandal to rhetoricians, they must put up with it. Another mood, another aspect:

> We are two that use these roses as we are,
> In seeing them.

Not as they are, but as we are. Stevens allows for the assertion that in seeing the roses, we two are changed. For the moment:

> This is what makes them seem
> So far beyond the rhetorician's touch.[50]

The emphatic "seem" steadies the line, and in such seemings all things are. Metaphor, not mentioned, will do its transforming work another day.

Notes

Acknowledgments

Index

Notes

Introduction

1. I. A. Richards, *Practical Criticism: A Study of Literary Judgment* (New York: Harcourt, Brace and World, 1929), p. 221.

2. T. S. Eliot, *Collected Poems 1909–1962* (London: Faber and Faber, 1974), pp. 77–78.

3. Cyril Tourneur, *The Revenger's Tragedy* (London: Nick Hern Books, 1996), pp. 54, 93.

4. Seamus Heaney, *Human Chain* (New York: Farrar, Straus and Giroux, 2010), p. 49.

5. J. Hillis Miller, *Others* (Princeton: Princeton University Press, 2001), p. 66.

6. James Wood, *The Irresponsible Self: On Laughter and the Self* (New York: Picador, 2005), p. 297.

7. T. S. Eliot, *On Poetry and Poets* (London: Faber and Faber, 1957), pp. 76–77.

8. Anonymous, "Roderick Hudson," *The Nation* (March 9, 1876), n.p.

9. Henry James, *Roderick Hudson* (New York: Read Books, Ltd., 2012, reprint of the 1st ed., 1875), ch. 11, p. 394.

10. Pierre A. Walker and Greg W. Zacharias, eds., *The Complete Letters of Henry James, 1872–1876,* vol. 3 (London and Lincoln: University of Nebraska Press, 2011), p. 90 (letter of March 31, 1876). I am indebted to James Wood, *How Fiction Works* (New York: Farrar, Straus and Giroux, 2008), p. 206, for this reference. We are both indebted to Philip Horne, ed., *Henry James: A Life in Letters* (New York: Viking Penguin, 1999), pp. 67–69.

Figure

Paul Ricoeur, *The Rule of Metaphor: The Creation of Meaning in Language,* trans. Robert Czerny with Kathleen McLaughlin and John Costello, SG (London and New York: Routledge Classics, 2003), p. 19.

1. James Joyce, *A Portrait of the Artist as a Young Man,* ed. Seamus Deane (London: Penguin Books, 1992), p. 35.

2. Ibid.

3. Ibid., p. 43.

4. Alan Bennett writes: "26 August: When I was religious as a boy I used to envy Catholics who only had to say the words of the Mass and not have to mean them in the way that Anglicans did" (*London Review of Books* 35, 1 [January 3, 2013]: 34). Not entirely true. We could not have translated the Latin, but we felt the communal experience, and the knowledge that all over the world Catholics, like us, were celebrating the Eucharist, in Latin. I can't comment on Anglicans.

5. Walter J. Ong, "Wit and Mystery: A Revaluation in Medieval Latin Hymnody," *Speculum* 22, no. 3 (July 1947): 310–341.

6. Ibid., 311.

7. T. S. Eliot, "Andrew Marvell," in *Selected Essays: New Edition* (New York: Harcourt, Brace and World, 1950), p. 252.

8. Guido Maria Dreves, ed., *Hymnographi Latini,* vol. 2 (Leipzig: Reisland, 1970), p. 586.

9. Peter G. Walsh, ed. and trans., with Christopher Husch, *One Hundred Latin Hymns: Ambrose to Aquinas* (Cambridge, MA: Harvard University Press, 2012), p. 365.

10. Ong, "Wit and Mystery," p. 317.

11. Hugh Kenner, "Rhyme: An Unfinished Monograph," *Common Knowledge* 10, no. 3 (2004): 424–425.

12. Roland Barthes, *The Preparation of the Novel,* trans. Kate Briggs (New York: Columbia University Press, 2011), p. 113.

13. Aquinas, "In Sententias Petri Lombardi Commentario," prolog., qu.1, a.5, ad 3. Quoted in Ong, "Wit and Mystery," p. 324.

14. Ong, "Wit and Mystery," pp. 324–325.

15. Aquinas, *Summa Theologiae* 1/1, trans. Thomas Gilby (London: Eyre and Spottiswood, 1964), p. 35. Quoted in Hans Blumenberg, *Paradigms for a Metaphorology,* trans. Robert Savage (Ithaca: Cornell University Press, 2010), p. 45.

16. Aquinas, *Summa Theologiae* 1/1, p. 35.

17. Hugh Kenner, "Rhyme: An Unfinished Monograph," *Common Knowledge* 10, no. 3 (2004): 424.

18. Walsh, *One Hundred Latin Hymns,* p. 367 (modified).

19. Ong, "Wit and Mystery," pp. 317–318, n. 30, citing Dom André Wilmart, "La tradition littéraire et textuelle de l'Adoro Te deuote," in *Recherches de théologie ancienne et médiévale,* vol. 1 (1929), p. 150.

20. Andrei Gotia, "Adoro Te Devote—A Synthesis of St. Thomas Aquinas's Eucharistic Theology," *Verbum* 6, no. 1 (2004): 112.

21. Robert Wielockx, "Poetry and Theology in the 'Adoro te deuote': Thomas Aquinas on the Eucharist and Christ's Uniqueness," in *Christ among the Medieval Dominicans: Representations of Christ in the Texts and Images of the Order of Preachers,* ed. Kent Emery Jr. and Joseph Wawrykow (Notre Dame: University of Notre Dame Press, 1998), p. 158.

22. Ibid.

23. Ibid., p. 167.

24. The fourth draft of Hopkins's "S. Thomae Aquinatis Rhythmus ad SS. Sacramentum" began:

Godhead here in hiding, whom I do adore
Masked by these bare shadows, shape and nothing more.

The final text begins:

Godhead, I adore thee fast in hiding; thou
God in these bare shapes, poor shadows, darkling now.

Cf. *Gerard Manley Hopkins,* ed. Catherine Phillips (Oxford: Oxford University Press, 1986), pp. 104 and 333.

25. Letter from Father John Saward to the author, March 19, 2010.

26. Walsh, *One Hundred Latin Hymns,* p. 365.

27. Erich Auerbach, "Figura," in *Scenes from the Drama of European Literature,* trans. Ralph Manheim (Minneapolis: University of Minnesota, 1984, reprint), p. 13.

28. Ibid., p. 30.

29. Cf. Garry Wills, "Catholics and Jews: The Great Change," *The New York Review of Books* 60, no. 5 (March 21, 2013): 36–37.

30. Joseph Ratzinger, "Pope Benedict XVI," in *Jesus of Nazareth: The Infancy Narratives,* trans. Philip J. Whitmore (New York: Image, 2012), p. 17.

31. Ibid., p. 51.

32. Cf. Wills, "Catholics and Jews," p. 36.

33. Ibid., p. 59.

34. Ibid., pp. 71–72.

35. Hans-Georg Gadamer, *Truth and Method* (London: Sheed and Ward, 2nd ed., 1979), p. 389.

36. John Henry Newman, *An Essay in Aid of a Grammar of Assent,* ed. I. T. Ker (Oxford: Clarendon Press, 1985), pp. 288–289.

37. Ibid., p. 289.

38. George Walton Williams, ed., *The Complete Poetry of Richard Crashaw* (New York: New York University Press, 1972), pp. 173–175.

39. Ibid., p. 177.

40. Hopkins, "S. Thomae Aquinatis Rhythmus ad SS. Sacramentum," p. 105.

41. Robert Alter, *The Book of Psalms* (New York: W. W. Norton, 2007), p. 354.

42. W. B. Yeats, *Essays and Introductions* (London: Macmillan, 1961), pp. 522–523.

43. T. H. White, ed., *The Bestiary: A Book of Beasts Being a Translation from a Latin Bestiary of the Twelfth Century* (New York: Putnam, 1954), pp. 132–133.

44. St. Thomas Aquinas, *Truth,* trans. Robert W. Schmidt, SJ, vol. 3 (Chicago: Henry Regnery, 1954), p. 104.

45. Blaise Pascal, *Pensées,* ed. Gérard Ferreyrolles and Philippe Sellier (Paris: Le Livre de Poche/Classiques Garnier, 1999), pp. 152 and 965.

46. Charles S. Hardwick, ed., *Semiotic and Significs: The Correspondence between Charles S. Peirce and Victoria Lady Welby* (Bloomington and London: Indiana University Press, 1977), letter of October 12, 1904, pp. 31–32.

47. Ricoeur, *The Rule of Metaphor,* p. 359.

48. Immanuel Kant, *Critique of the Faculty of Judgment,* trans. James Creed Meredith (Oxford: Clarendon Press, 1952), pp. 175–176.

49. Gaston Bachelard, *Air and Dreams: An Essay on the Imagination of Movement,* trans. Edith R. Farrell and C. Frederick Farrell (Dallas: Dallas Institute of Humanities and Culture, 1988), p. 72 (emphases in the original). Quoted in Barthes, *The Preparation of the Novel,* pp. 16 and 412.

50. Wallace Stevens, *The Necessary Angel: Essays on Reality and the Imagination* (New York: Knopf, 1951), p. 7.

After Aristotle

William Empson, *The Structure of Complex Words* (London: The Hogarth Press, 1985 reprint of 1951 ed.), p. 339.

1. Gustav Stern, *Meaning and Change of Meaning with Special Reference to the English Language* (Göteborg: Elanders Boktryckeri Aktiebolag, 1931), pp. 298–300.

2. Ibid., p. 308.

3. Vladimir Nabokov, *Despair* (New York: Vintage International, 1989 reprint), pp. 5–6.

4. Ibid., p. 89.

5. Empson, *Structure,* p. 335.

6. Friedrich Nietzsche, "On Truth and Lies in a Normal Sense," in *Philosophy and Truth: Selections from Nietzsche's Notebooks of the Early 1870s,* trans. and ed. Daniel Breazeale (Atlantic Highlands, NJ: Humanities Press, 1979), p. 84.

7. Karl Kraus, *Die dritte Walpurgisnacht* (Munich: Kösel, 1952), p. 122. Quoted in Roberto Calasso, *K,* trans. Geoffrey Brock (New York: Knopf, 2005), p. 95.

8. Samuel Taylor Coleridge, *Lectures 1795 on Politics and Religion,* ed. Lewis Patton and Peter Mann (Princeton: Princeton University Press, 1971), p. 202.

9. Samuel Taylor Coleridge, *Notebooks,* ed. Kathleen Coburn, vol. 1 (London: Routledge and Kegan Paul, 1962), p. 2710, n. 2711.

10. Gerald F. Else, trans., *Aristotle's Poetics* (Ann Arbor: University of Michigan Press, Ann Arbor Paperback, 1970), p. 9

11. Cf. Ismail M. Dahiyat, *Avicenna's Commentary on the Poetics of Aristotle* (Leiden: E. J. Brill, 1974), pp. ix, 9ff.

12. S. H. Butcher, trans., *Aristotle's Poetics* (New York: Hill and Wang, 1966, reprint), pp. 99–100, 103–104.

13. Hannah Arendt, *Thinking,* vol. 1 of *The Life of the Mind* (New York and London: Harcourt Brace Jovanovich, 1978), pp. 104–105.

14. Aristotle, *On Rhetoric,* bk. 3, ch. 11, 1412a, trans. George A. Kennedy (New York: Oxford University Press, 1991), pp. 248–249.

15. Christine Brooke-Rose, *A Grammar of Metaphor* (London: Secker and Warburg, 1958), p. 206.

16. Samuel Taylor Coleridge, *The Friend,* ed. Barbara E. Rooke, vol. 2 (Princeton: Princeton University Press, 1969), p. 280; first published January 11, 1810.

17. A. W. Schlegel, "Kritische Schriften und Briefe, II. 51," in David Simpson, *Irony and Authority in Romantic Poetry* (Totowa, NJ: Rowman and Littlefield, 1979), p. 158.

18. Paul Ricoeur, *The Rule of Metaphor: The Creation of Meaning in Language,* trans. Robert Czerny with Kathleen McLaughlin and John Costello, SJ (London and New York: Routledge Classics, 2003), p. 20.

19. Ibid., p. 302.

20. Aristotle, *De Anima,* trans. R. D. Hicks (New York: Cosimo Classics, 2008), p. 82.

21. Aristotle, *On the Soul,* trans. W. S. Hett (Cambridge, MA: Harvard University Press, 1964), p. xiii.

22. M. Schofield, "Aristotle on the Imagination," in *Aristotle on Mind and the Senses,* ed. G. E. R. Lloyd and G. E. L. Owen (Cambridge: Cambridge University Press, 1978), p. 116.

23. G. E. R. Lloyd, *The Revolutions of Wisdom: Studies in the Claims and Practice of Ancient Greek Science* (Berkeley: University of California Press, 1987), p. 211.

24. John Donne, *The Complete English Poems,* ed. A. J. Smith (New York: St. Martin's Press, 1971), p. 372.

25. Samuel Beckett, *Worstward Ho* (London: John Calder, 1983), p. 45.

26. George Saunders, *Pastoralia* (New York: Riverhead Books, 2000), p. 137.

27. Gaston Bachelard, *The Poetics of Reverie: Childhood, Language, and the Cosmos,* trans. Daniel Russell (Boston: Beacon Press, 1971), p. 7.

28. Michael Silk, "Metaphor and Metonymy: Aristotle, Jakobson, Ricoeur, and Others," in *Metaphor, Allegory, and the Classical Tradition: Ancient Thought and Modern Revision,* ed. G. R. Boys-Stones (Oxford: Oxford University Press, 2003), p. 132.

29. Roman Jakobson, "Two Aspects of Language and Two Types of Aphasic Disturbances," in *Language in Literature,* ed. Krystyna Pomorska and Stephen Rudy (Cambridge, MA: Belknap Press of Harvard University Press, 1987), p. 111.

30. George Lakoff and Mark Johnson, *Metaphors We Live By* (Chicago: University of Chicago Press, 2003), pp. 38–39.

31. Elizabeth Bishop, "In the Waiting Room," in *The Complete Poems 1927–1979* (New York: Farrar, Straus, and Giroux. 1983), p. 159.

32. T. S. Eliot, "The Love Song of J. Alfred Prufrock," in *Collected Poems 1909–1962* (New York: Harcourt Brace and Company, 1963), p. 3.

33. Stanley Fish, *Surprised by Sin: The Reader in Paradise Lost* (Berkeley: University of California Press, 1971), p. 25.

34. Virginia Woolf, *The Waves,* annot. Molly Hite (Orlando: Harcourt, 2006), p. 14.

35. *The Poems of John Keats,* ed. Miriam Allott (London: Longman, 1970), p. 104.

36. G. W. F. Hegel, *Aesthetics: Lectures on Fine Art,* trans. T. M. Knox, vol. 1 (Oxford: Clarendon Press, 1975), p. 411.

37. Aristotle, *On Rhetoric,* bk. 3, 1406b–1407a.

38. John Middleton Murry, "Metaphor," in *Countries of the Mind: Essays in Literary Criticism,* 2nd series, 1931, reprinted in *Shakespeare Criticism 1919–35,* ed. Anne Bradby (London: Oxford University Press, 1936), p. 228.

39. Ibid.

40. Hegel, *Aesthetics,* p. 407.

41. Ibid., p. 405.

42. Joseph Conrad, *Lord Jim: A Tale,* ed. Jacques Berthoud (New York: Oxford University Press, 2002 reprint), pp. 53–54, 58, 67.

43. Howard Nemerov, *Reflexions on Poetry and Poetics* (New Brunswick: Rutgers University Press, 1972), pp. 34–35.

44. Northrop Frye, *Myth and Metaphor: Selected Essays 1974–1988,* ed. Robert D. Denham (Charlottesville: University Press of Virginia, 1990), p. 118.

45. Christine Brooke-Rose, *A Grammar of Metaphor* (London: Secker and Warburg, 1958), p. 9. Cf. I. A. Richards, *The Philosophy of Rhetoric* (New York and London: Oxford University Press, 1936), pp. 96 and 120–121.

46. Shakespeare, Sonnet 73 in *Shakespeare's Sonnets,* ed. Stephen Booth (New Haven: Yale University Press, 1977), p. 64.

47. John Donne, *The Complete Poetry and Selected Prose,* ed. Charles M. Coffin (New York: The Modern Library, 2001), p. 40.

48. Kenneth Burke, *Permanence and Change: An Anatomy of Purpose* (Los Altos, CA: Hermes Publications, rev. ed., 1954), p. 89.

49. Donne, "The Canonization," *The Complete Poetry and Selected Prose,* p. 13.

50. Ian McEwan, *Solar: A Novel* (New York: Nan A. Talese/Doubleday, 2010), p. 61.

51. Heinrich Lausberg, *Handbook of Literary Rhetoric: A Foundation for Literary Study,* trans. Matthew T. Bliss, Annemiek Jansen, and David E. Orton (Leiden: Brill, 1998), p. 251.

52. *The New Science of Giambattista Vico,* trans. Thomas Goddard Bergin and Max Harold Fisch (Ithaca: Cornell University Press, 1968), section 31, p. 20.

53. I owe this to Aldo D'Alfonso, "Metaphor and Language Learning: A Vichian Perspective," in *Giambattista Vico and Anglo-American Science: Philosophy and Writing,* ed. Marcel Danesi (Berlin: Mouton de Gruyter, 1995), p. 53.

No Resemblance

Virginia Woolf, *The Waves* (Orlando: Harcourt, 2006), p. 118.

1. James Joyce, *A Portrait of the Artist as a Young Man,* ed. Seamus Deane (London: Penguin Books, 1992), p. 35.

2. William Empson, *Seven Types of Ambiguity* (London: Chatto and Windus, 3rd ed., 1953), pp. 23–25.

3. I. A. Richards, *The Philosophy of Rhetoric* (London: Oxford University Press, 1965, reprint), pp. 124–125.

4. Empson, *Seven Types of Ambiguity,* p. 109.

5. Richards, *Philosophy of Rhetoric,* p. 127.

6. Stephen Booth, ed. (with analytic commentary), *Shakespeare's Sonnets* (New Haven: Yale University Press, 2000, reprint), p. 239.

7. George Herbert: "Prayer (I)": *The Complete English Poems,* ed. John Tobin (London: Penguin Books, 2004), pp. 45–46.

8. Henry Vaughan, *The Complete Poems,* ed. Ian Rudrum (New Haven: Yale University Press, 1981), p. 290.

9. Donald Davie, *Articulate Energy: An Inquiry into the Syntax of English Poetry* (London: Routledge and Kegan Paul, 1955), p. 48.

10. John Keats, *Selected Poems and Letters,* ed. Douglas Bush (Boston: Houghton Mifflin, 1959), p. 162.

11. Arthur Rimbaud, *Oeuvres,* ed. Suzanne Bernard (Paris: Garnier, 1960), p. 129.

12. Arthur Rimbaud, *Selected Poems and Letters,* trans. Jeremy Harding and John Sturrock (London: Penguin Books, 2004), p. 89.

13. Hugo Friedrich, *The Structure of Modern Poetry,* trans. Joachim Neugroschel (Evanston: Northwestern University Press, 1974), pp. 57, 93.

14. Hans Blumenberg, *Paradigms for a Metaphorology,* trans. Robert Savage (Ithaca: Cornell University Press, 2010), p. 78.

15. Roberto Calasso, *Literature and the Gods,* trans. Tim Parks (New York: Vintage, 2001), p. 129.

16. Ezra Pound, *Collected Shorter Poems* (London: Faber and Faber, second edition, 1968), p. 222.

17. Hugh Kenner, *The Pound Era* (Berkeley and Los Angeles: University of California Press, 1971), p. 288.

18. S. Reinach, *Apollo: An Illustrated Manual of the History of Art throughout the Ages,* trans. Florence Simmonds (New York: Scribner's; London: Heinemann, 1912 edition), pp. 189–191.

19. John Keats, *Poetical Works,* ed. H. W. Garrod (Oxford: Clarendon Press, 1939), p. 260.

20. Miriam Allott, ed., *The Poems of John Keats* (London: Longman, 1970), pp. 533–534.

21. Cf. Kenneth Burke, *A Grammar of Motives and a Rhetoric of Motives* (Cleveland and New York: World Publishing Company, 1962), p. 448.

22. George Steiner, *The Poetry of Thought: From Hellenism to Celan* (New York: New Directions, 2011), pp. 158–159.

23. Helen Vendler, *The Odes of John Keats* (Cambridge, MA: Belknap Press of Harvard University Press, 1983), pp. 145–146.

24. John Jones, *John Keats's Dream of Truth* (New York: Barnes and Noble, 1969), p. 220.

25. John Locke, *An Essay Concerning Human Understanding,* ed. Peter H. Nedditch (Oxford: Clarendon Press, 1975), p. 395.

26. William Hazlitt, *Works,* ed. P. P. Howe, vol. 1 (London: Dent, 1930–1934), p. 73.

27. Samuel Taylor Coleridge, *Biographia Literaria,* ed. James Engell and W. Jackson Bate, vol. 1 (Princeton: Princeton University Press, 1983), p. 116.

28. C. S. Peirce, *Selected Writings,* ed. Philip P. Wiener (Stanford: Stanford University Press, 1958), p. 67.

29. Remy de Gourmont, *Selected Writings,* ed. Glenn S. Burne (Ann Arbor: University of Michigan Press, 1966), p. 15.

30. W. B. Yeats, *Essays and Introductions* (London: Macmillan, 1961), p. 405.

31. Quoted in Richards, *Philosophy of Rhetoric,* p. 123.

32. Ibid., p. 126.

33. Roland Barthes, *The Preparation of the Novel,* trans. Kate Briggs (New York: Columbia University Press, 2011), p. 120.

34. Frederick Seidel, "Moto Poeta," *The New York Review of Books* 59, no. 14 (September 27, 2012): 58.

"It Ensures That Nothing Goes without a Name"

Julian Jaynes, *The Origin of Consciousness in the Breakdown of the Bicameral Mind* (Boston: Houghton Mifflin, 1977), p. 48.

Ernest Fenollosa and Ezra Pound, *The Chinese Written Character as a Medium for Poetry,* ed. Haun Saussy, Jonathan Stalling, and Lucas Klein (New York: Fordham University Press, 2008), pp. 54–55.

Ezra Pound, *The Chinese Written Character as a Medium for Poetry,* p. 55.

1. Cf. Hans Aarsleff, *From Locke to Saussure: Essays on the Study of Language and Intellectual History* (Minneapolis: University of Minnesota Press, 1982), p. 42ff.

2. Thomas Goddard Bergin and Max Harold Fisch, trans. (from the 3rd ed. [1744]) *The New Science of Giambattista Vico* (Ithaca: Cornell University Press, 1948), p. 138.

3. Étienne Bonnot and Abbé de Condillac, *Oeuvres philosophiques de Condillac,* ed. Georges le Roy, vol. 1 (Paris: Presses Universitaires de France, 1947–1951), p. 101. Quoted in Hans Aarsleff, *From Locke to Saussure: Essays on the Study of Language and Intellectual History* (Minneapolis: University of Minnesota Press, 1982), p. 166.

4. Jean-Jacques Rousseau, *Essay on the Origin of Languages and Writings Related to Music,* trans. John T. Scott (Hanover and London: University Press of New England, 1998), pp. 293–294.

5. Kenneth Burke, *A Grammar of Motives and a Rhetoric of Motives* (Cleveland and New York: World Publishing Company, 1962), p. 503.

6. G. W. F. Hegel, *Phenomenology of Spirit,* trans. A. V. Miller (Oxford: Oxford University Press, 1977), p. 58.

7. Ibid.

8. Herbert Eveleth Greene, *A Grouping of Figures of Speech Based upon the Principle of Their Effectiveness* (Baltimore: The Modern Language Association of America, 1893), p. 10.

9. J. L. Austin, *Sense and Sensibilia,* reconstr. G. J. Warnock (Oxford: Oxford University Press, 1962), p. 75.

10. James Joyce, *Ulysses,* ed. Hans Walter Gabler, Wolfhard Steppe, and Claus Melchior (New York: Random House, 1986), p. 283.

11. Jacques Derrida, *Writing and Difference,* trans. Alan Bass (Chicago: University of Chicago Press, 1978), p. 4.

12. Ernst Cassirer, *Mythical Thought,* vol. 2 of *The Philosophy of Symbolic Forms,* trans. Ralph Manheim (New Haven: Yale University Press, 1955), p. xvi.

13. Ibid., p. 34.

14. Ibid.

15. Dante, *The Divine Comedy: Inferno,* trans. Charles S. Singleton (Princeton: Princeton University Press, 1970), Canto 15, line 21, pp. 154–155.

16. Percy Bysshe Shelley, *Complete Works: Poems,* vol. 4 (New York: Scribner, 1928), p. 59.

17. Roman Jakobson, *Language in Literature,* ed. Krystyna Pomortska (Cambridge, MA: The Belknap Press of Harvard University Press, 1987), p. 25.

18. Leo Tolstoy, *Anna Karenina,* trans. Richard Pevear and Larissa Volokhonsky (New York: Penguin Books, 2000), p. 768.

19. César Chesneau du Marsais, *Les Tropes,* vol. 1 (Geneva: Slatkine Reprints, 1967), pp. 76–103.

20. Richard A. Lanham, *A Handlist of Rhetorical Terms* (Berkeley: University of California Press, 1969), pp. 76–77.

21. Brian Vickers, *In Defence of Rhetoric* (Oxford: Clarendon Press, 1988), p. 445.

22. Du Marsais, *Les Tropes,* vol. 11, p. 87.

23. Kenneth Burke, *A Grammar of Motives and a Rhetoric of Motives* (Cleveland and New York: World Publishing Company, 1962), p. 506.

24. Gérard Genette, *Figures III* (Paris: Éditions du Seuil, 1972), p. 55.

25. Franz Kafka, *The Diaries of Franz Kafka 1914–1923,* ed. Max Brod and trans. Martin Greenberg (New York: Schocken Books, 1949), pp. 200–201.

26. Pierre Fontanier, *Les Figures du discourse,* ed. Gérard Ginette (Paris: Flammarion, 1968), pp. 145–146.

27. Søren Kierkegaard, *The Concept of Irony,* trans. Lee M. Capel (Bloomington: Indiana University Press, 1971), pp. 270, 273.

28. Marcel Proust, *A la recherche du temps perdu,* vol. 1 (Paris: Gallimard, 1954), p. 211.

29. Cicero, *De Oratore,* 2.67. Cf. Gregory Vlastos, *Socrates, Ironist and Moral Philosopher* (Ithaca: Cornell University Press, 1991), p. 28.

30. Cf. Marvin Mudrick, *Jane Austen: Irony as Defense and Discovery* (Berkeley: University of California Press, 1968), p. 3.

31. H. W. F[owler], "Irony of Fate," in *S. P. E. Tract no. 13* (Oxford: Clarendon Press, 1923), p. 33.

32. Ibid., p. 34.

33. Kierkegaard, *The Concept of Irony,* p. 49.

34. Ibid., pp. 270, 271, 265, 296–297.

35. Walter Pater, *Marius the Epicurean: His Sensations and Ideas,* vol. 1 (London: Macmillan, 1910, reprint), p. 133.

36. Nate Silver: "Nate Silver Solves the Swing-State Puzzle!," *The New York Times Magazine,* September 23, 2012, p. 17.

Not Quite against Metaphor

Dante, *Dantis Alagherii Epistolae,* ed. and trans. Paget Toynbee (Oxford: Clarendon Press, 2nd ed., 1966), *Epistola* 10, p. 29.

J. L. Austin, *Philosophical Papers,* ed. J. O. Urmson and G. J. Warnock (Oxford: Oxford University Press, 3rd. ed., 1979), p. 68.

Paul de Man, *Allegories of Reading: Figural Language in Rousseau, Nietzsche, Rilke, and Proust* (New Haven and London: Yale University Press, 1979), p. 5.

1. Franz Kafka, *Briefe 1902–1924* (New York: Schocken Books, 1958), p. 364.

2. Franz Kafka, *Diaries, 1910–1923,* trans. Joseph Kresh and by Martin Greenberg with the cooperation of Hannah Arendt, ed. Max Brod (New York: Schocken Books, 1976, reprint), pp. 397–398.

3. Walter Benjamin, *The Origin of German Tragic Drama,* trans. John Osborne (London: Verso, 1998), p. 166.

4. Robert Mankin: "An Introduction to *The Claim of Reason,*" *Salmagundi* 67 (Summer 1985): 77.

5. Ibid.

6. Stanley Cavell, *In Quest of the Ordinary: Lines of Skepticism and Romanticism* (Chicago: University of Chicago Press, 1988), p. 146.

7. Ibid., pp. 146–147.

8. Ibid., p. 149.

9. Stanley Cavell, *The Claim of Reason: Wittgenstein, Skepticism, Morality, and Tragedy* (New York: Oxford University Press, 1999), pp. 168–169.

10. Ibid., pp. 189–190.

11. Don De Lillo, *White Noise* (New York: Penguin Books, 1986), p. 32.

12. Austin, *Philosophical Papers,* p. 185.

13. Stanley Cavell: "Austin at Criticism," in *Symposium on J. L. Austin,* ed. K. T. Fann (London: Routledge and Kegan Paul, 1969), p. 61.

14. J. L. Austin, *How to Do Things with Words* (London: Oxford University Press, 1962), p. 22.

15. Jacques Derrida, *Limited Inc* (Evanston: Northwestern University Press, 1988), p. 16ff.

16. Stanley Fish, "How Ordinary Is Ordinary Language?," *New Literary History* 5, no. 1 (Autumn 1973): 41.

17. John Searle, "Chomsky's Revolution in Lingui," *The New York Review of Books* (June 29, 1972): 23.

18. Fish, "How Ordinary Is Ordinary Language?," p. 52.

19. Ibid.

20. Harold Bloom, "Criticism, Canon-Formation, and Prophecy," *Raritan* (Winter 1984): 3.

21. Hannah Arendt, *The Life of the Mind: One: Thinking* (New York: Harcourt Brace Jovanovich, 1978), pp. 112–113.

22. George Eliot, *Middlemarch* (Oxford: Oxford University Press, 1988, reprint), pp. 69–70.

23. J. Hillis Miller, *Reading for Our Time: "Adam Bede" and "Middlemarch" Revisited* (Edinburgh: Edinburgh University Press, 2012), p. 53.

24. George Eliot, *Middlemarch,* bk. 1, ch. 5, p. 36.

25. Ibid, bk. 1, ch. 20, p. 59.

26. Miller, *Reading for Our Time,* p. 131.

27. George Lakoff and Mark Johnson, *Metaphors We Live By* (Chicago: University of Chicago Press, 1980), p. 4.

28. Brian Vickers, *In Defence of Rhetoric* (Oxford: Clarendon Press, 1988), p. 445.

29. Lakoff and Johnson, *Metaphors,* p. 230.

30. Wallace Stevens, *Collected Poems* (New York: Knopf, 1954), pp. 430–431.

31. Gérard Genette, *Figures of Literary Discourse,* trans. Alan Sheridan (New York: Columbia University Press, 1982), p. 113. Cf. Genette, "Metonymie chez Proust," in *Figures III* (Paris: Seuil, 1972), pp. 41–63.

32. Ibid., p. 117.

33. Ibid., p. 122, n. 7.

34. Ibid., p. 125, n. 36.

35. Gérard Genette, *Figures III* (Paris: Seuil, 1972), p. 55.

36. Marcel Proust, *A La Recherche du Temps Perdu,* ed. Pierre Clarac and André, vol. 3 (Paris: Gallimard, 1954), p. 889.

37. Proust, *Time Regained,* vol. 6 of *In Search of Lost Time,* trans. Andreas Mayor and Terence Kilmartin, rev. D. J. Enright (New York: The Modern Library, 2003), pp. 289–290.

38. Genette, *Figures of Literary Discourse,* p. 214.

39. Paul Ricoeur, *The Rule of Metaphor: The Creation of Meaning in Language,* trans. Robert Czerny with Kathleen McLaughlin and John Costello, SJ (London and New York: Routledge Classics, 2003), p. 219.

40. Ibid., p. 220.

41. Marcel Proust, *Essais et articles* (Paris: Gallimard, 1971), p. 586.

42. Genette, *Figures of Literary Discourse,* p. 208.

43. Bernard Lamy, *La Rhétorique, ou L'art de parler* (Amsterdam: 4th ed., 1699), p. 285.

44. Roberto Calasso, *La Folie Baudelaire,* trans. Alastair McEwen (New York: Farrar, Straus and Giroux, 2012), p. 140.

45. Cf. Michael Riffaterre, *Semiotics of Poetry* (Bloomington and London: Indiana University Press, 1978), pp. 122–124.

46. Gérard Genette, "Métonymie chez Proust," in *Figures III* (Paris: Seuil, 1972), p. 55.

47. Ibid., p. 63.

48. Pierre Fontanier, *Les Figures du discours,* ed. Gérard Ginette (Paris: Flammarion, 1968), p. 404ff. Quoted in Michael Riffaterre, "Prosopopeia," *Yale French Studies* 69 (1985): 107.

49. Paul de Man, *The Rhetoric of Romanticism* (New York: Columbia University Press, 1984), p. 77.

50. Paul de Man, "Hypogram and Inscription" (1981), in *The Resistance to Theory* (Minneapolis: University of Minnesota Press, 1986), pp. 45, 48.

51. Ibid., p. 47.

52. Victor Hugo, *Les Rayons et les ombres,* ed. Pierre Albouy, vol. 1 (Paris: Gallimard, 1964), lines 1062–1063.

53. Michael Riffaterre, *Textual Production,* trans. Terese Lyons (New York: Columbia University Press, 1983), p. 183.

54. Ibid., p. 201.

55. De Man, *The Resistance to Theory,* p. 47.

56. Ibid., p. 49.

57. Ibid., pp 49–50.

58. Thomas Hardy, *Complete Poems,* ed. James Gibson (London: Macmillan, 1976), p. 346.

59. Samuel Beckett, *The Collected Shorter Plays* (London: Faber and Faber, 1984), p. 132.

The Motive for Metaphor

Jacques Derrida, "White Mythology": *Margins of Philosophy,* trans. Alan Bass (Chicago: University of Chicago, 1982), p. 215.

1. W. B. Yeats, *Variorum Edition of the Poems,* ed. Peter Allt and Russell K. Alspach (New York: Macmillan, 1957), p. 475.

2. Hans Blumenberg, "An Anthropological Approach to the Contemporary Significance of Rhetoric," in *After Philosophy: End or Transformation?,* ed. Kenneth Baynes, James Bohman, and Thomas McCarthy (Cambridge, MA: MIT Press, 1987), p. 447.

3. Pierre Fontanier, *Les Figures du Discours,* ed. Gérard Ginette (Paris: Flammarion, 1968), p. 116.

4. Ibid., p. 213ff.

5. Ibid., p. 216.

6. Paul de Man: "The Epistemology of Metaphor," in *On Metaphor,* ed. Sheldon Sacks (Chicago: University of Chicago Press, 1979), p. 19.

7. Robert Frost, *Collected Poems, Prose, and Plays* (New York: Library of America, 1995), p. 341.

8. Wallace Stevens, *Collected Poems* (New York: Knopf, 1954), p. 288.

9. Northrop Frye, *The Educated Imagination and Other Writings on Critical Theory 1933–1963,* ed. Germaine Warkentin, vol. 21 (Toronto: University of Toronto Press, 2006), pp. 445–446.

10. John Crowe Ransom, *Poems and Essays* (New York: Vintage Books, 1955), pp. 178–179.

11. Shakespeare, Sonnet 111, in *Shakespeare's Sonnets,* ed. Stephen Booth (New Haven: Yale University Press, 2000), p. 96.

12. Stevens, *Opus Posthumous,* ed. Milton J. Bates (New York: Knopf, 1989), p. 195.

13. G. W. F. Hegel, *Aesthetics: Lectures on Fine Art,* trans. T. M. Knox, vol. 1 (Oxford: Clarendon Press, 1975), pp. 31–32.

14. Stevens, "The Pure Good of Theory," *Collected Poems,* p. 331.

15. Stevens, "Description without Place," *Collected Poems,* p. 353.

16. Stevens, "Notes toward a Supreme Fiction," *Collected Poems,* p. 353.

17. Stevens, *Collected Poems,* p. 471.

18. Quoted in Stevens, "The Noble Rider and the Sound of Words," in *The Necessary Angel: Essays on Reality and the Imagination* (New York: Knopf, 1951), p. 30.

19. Stevens, *The Necessary Angel,* pp. 174–175.

20. Ibid., p. 161.

21. José Ortega y Gasset, *The Dehumanization of Art and Other Writings on Art and Culture* (Garden City, NJ: Doubleday Anchor Books, n.d.), pp. 30–31.

22. Cf. Harold Bloom, *Wallace Stevens: The Poems of Our Climate* (Ithaca: Cornell University Press, 1977), p. 322.

23. Wallace Stevens, *The Palm at the End of the Mind*, ed. Holly Stevens (New York: Vintage Books, 1990), pp. 295–296.

24. Stevens, "The Creations of Sound," *Collected Poems*, pp. 310–311.

25. William Hazlitt, "Character of Mr. Wordsworth's New Poem, The Excursion" (1814): *The Complete Works*, ed. P. P. Howe (London: Dent, 1933), pp. 11–13.

26. Helen Vendler, *Wallace Stevens: Words Chosen Out of Desire* (Knoxville: University of Tennessee Press, 1984), pp. 23–26.

27. *Letters of Wallace Stevens*, ed. Holly Stevens (Berkeley: University of California Press, 1996 reprint), letter of June 19, 1951, p. 719.

28. Stevens, "Credences of Summer," *Collected Poems*, p. 373.

29. Stevens, "Esthétique du Mal," *Collected Poems*, p. 314.

30. Stevens, "Thinking of a Relation between the Images of Metaphors," *Collected Poems*, p. 356.

31. Stevens, *The Necessary Angel*, p. 122.

32. Ibid., p. 48.

33. Stevens, "Description without Place," *Collected Poems*, p. 341.

34. Stevens, "Three Academic Pieces," *The Necessary Angel*, pp. 71–72.

35. Ibid., p. 75.

36. Aristotle, *Metaphysics*, trans. Hugh Tredennich (Cambridge, MA: Harvard University Press, 1968 reprint), bk. 5 ch. 9, 1018 a 15–20, p. 243.

37. Max Black, *Models and Metaphors* (Ithaca: Cornell University Press, 1962), p. 37. Nelson Goodman, *Languages of Art: An Approach to a Theory of Symbols* (New York: Bobbs-Merrill, 1968), p. 78.

38. Nelson Goodman, *Problems and Projects* (Indianapolis and New York: Bobbs-Merrill, 1972), pp. 437–446.

39. Stevens, *The Necessary Angel*, p. 77.

40. Ibid., pp. 77–78.

41. Stevens, *The Palm at the End of the Mind*, p. 299.

42. Goodman, *Languages of Art*, p. 69.

43. Stevens, *Collected Poems*, pp. 468–469.

44. Ibid., p. 476.

45. Shelley, "A Defence of Poetry," *Shelley's Critical Prose*, ed. by Bruce R. McElderry Jr. (Lincoln: University of Nebraska Press, 1967), p. 6.

46. Stevens, *Opus Posthumous*, p. 205.
47. Stevens, *Collected Poems*, pp. 444–445.
48. Stevens, "The Owl in the Sarcophagus," *Collected Poems*, p. 436.
49. Stevens, "The Bouquet," *Collected Poems*, p. 451.
50. Stevens," Bouquet of Roses in Sunlight," *Collected Poems*, pp. 430–431.

Acknowledgments

Thanks to James Applewhite, Peter Burian, Andrei Gotia, Richard Lehan, W. J. McCormack, Thomas McGonigle, Melissa Malouf, Sergio Perosa, and Father John Saward.

I am also grateful to Paula Deitz for permission to use "The Motive for Metaphor," a version of which was published in *The Hudson Review* 65, no. 4 (Winter 2013).

Index

Absolute metaphor. *See* Autonomous
  metaphor
Aeneid (Virgil), 72
Alter, Robert, 44
Anna Karenina (Tolstoy), 129–130
Antony and Cleopatra (Shakespeare), 3, 56,
  81, 86–87
Aquinas, St. Thomas, 15, 18–20, 21–29,
  41–42, 46–47
Arendt, Hannah, 62–63, 159–160
Aristotle, 59–60, 61–63, 98–100, 122,
  199; opinion of metaphor, 65–68;
  comparison of simile and metaphor,
  80; on irony, 137
"As," contrasted with "like," 105
Association, of incompatible notions,
  111–117; in metonymy, 166–167
Auerbach, Erich, 29, 30–40
Augustine, St., 34
Austin, J. L., 125, 152–154
Autonomous metaphor, 106; "Ode on a
  Grecian Urn" as example of, 106–111

Bachelard, Gaston, 48–49, 72
Barthes, Roland, 21, 95, 116
Beckett, Samuel, 54, 69–70, 181
Biographia Literaria (Coleridge), 60,
  113
Blumenberg, Hans, 101, 184
Burke, Kenneth, 86, 122–123, 132

Calasso, Roberto, 174
Cassirer, Ernst, 126–127
Catachresis, 111, 184–185
Catullus, 30
Cavell, Stanley, 141; and ordinary versus
  figurative language, 146–155

Christian perspectives of metaphor,
  21–29, 31–40
Cicero, 29–30, 131, 133, 137
Coleridge, Samuel Taylor, 57–58, 60, 64,
  113, 142
Common usage of language. *See* ordinary
  language
Conrad, Joseph, 82–83
Coriolanus (Shakespeare), 167
Crashaw, Richard, 41–42
Cymbeline (Shakespeare), 140–141

Dante, 38–39, 44, 127
De Anima (Aristotle), 67
De Man, Paul, 175–181, 185
Despair (Nabokov), 53–54
Dissimilarity in metaphor, 99–102.
  See also Autonomous metaphor
Donne, John, 69, 86
Du Marsais, Cesar Chesneau, 131,
  134

Eliot, T. S. (Thomas Stearns), 18, 75
Extended metaphor, 70–71

Figure, 20; theological use, 23–28;
  origins of term in ancient world.
  29–31; in the Christian world, 31–40,
  49–51
Fish, Stanley, 77; on ordinary versus
  figurative language, 155–158
Fontanier, Pierre, 132, 134, 136, 175,
  184–185
Fowler, H. W., 138–139
Free indirect style, 70–71
Friedrich, Hugo, 100

Frost, Robert, 57, 84
Frye, Northrup, 84, 186, 187

Gadamer, Hans-Georg, 39
Genesis, 119–120
Genette, Gerard, 132, 170–175; on Proust and metaphor, 170–173
Goodman, Nelson, 199
Gotia, Andrei, 25

Hamlet (Shakespeare), 44
Hardy, Thomas, 180
Hegel, G. W. F., 78–79, 123–124; on difference between simile and metaphor, 82; the Universal and, 186–187, 188–189, 205–206
Henry V (Shakespeare), 4
Herbert, George, 96–97
Hopkins, Gerard Manley, 41, 43

Idea of a University, The (Newman), 60–61
"In Memory of Stephen A. Aaron (1936–2012)" (Seidel), 116–117
Irony, 136–142; Vico on, 90, 138; Kierkegaard on, 137, 139–140; conventional use of language and, 140–142

Jakobson, Roman, 73, 129
James, Henry, 10–11
Johnson, Mark, 164–168
Jones, John, 110
Julius Caesar (Shakespeare), 125

Kant, Immanuel, 48
Keats, John, 77–78, 99, 106–111, 115–116
Kenner, Hugh, 19–20, 23–24
Kierkegaard, Soren: on irony, 137, 139–140
King Lear (Shakespeare), 45
Kraus, Karl, 57

Lakoff, George, 164–168
Latin verse, 15–29
"Like," contrasted with "as," 105
Likeness. *See* resemblance
Literature and ordinary language, 155–158
Locke, John, 112, 120
Longinus, 30, 59, 66, 99–100
Lord Jim (Conrad), 82–83
Lucretius, 29–30

Macbeth (Shakespeare), 8
Mankin, Robert, 146–149
McEwan, Ian, 87
Metaphor: definition, 1–5, 52; personification, contrasted with, 6–7; mixed, 8; theology and, 21–29, 31–40; pelican as, 43–48; distinct from simile, 53–54, 80–82; diminishing of through common usage, 55–56; distinction between reality and, 57–59; Aristotle's definition, 61–62; resemblance as factor in, 61–68; slow and quick, 69–70; extended, 70–71; contrasted with metonymy, 74, 82–83, 132; Vico on, 89; dissimilarity in, 99–102; autonomous metaphor, 106–111; and concept of association, 111–117; Kafka's despair over, 135–136, 144–146; Austin on, 153–154; Arendt on, 159–160; Lakoff and Johnson on, 164–168; Proust's use of, 170–173; prosopopeia as alternative to, 175–181; Stevens's bizarre examples of, 201–204
"Medallion" (Pound), 102–106
Metonymy, 71–74; contrasted with realism, 73; contrasted with metaphor, 74, 82–83, 132; Vico on, 90, 122–123; definition, 128; association between elements, 128–129, 166–167; contrasted with synecdoche, 130–131, 134
Middlemarch (Eliot), 160–164
Miller, J. Hillis, 5
Milton, John, 50, 76
Mixed metaphor, 8

"Motive for Metaphor, The" (Stevens), 191–197
Murry, John Middleton, 80–81

Nabokov, Vladimir, 53–54
Newman, John Henry, 39–40, 60–61
New Science, The (Vico), 87–91
New Testament, relationship to Old, 32–39, 49–51
Nietzsche, Friedrich, 55–56, 159, 191
Norton, Grace, 10–11

"Ode on a Grecian Urn" (Keats): as autonomous metaphor, 106–111, 115–116
Old Testament, supercession of by New, 32–39, 49–51
Ong, Fr. Walter J., 17–18, 21, 23, 25
On Translating Homer (Arnold), 60, 61
Ordinary language: metaphors and, 55–56; irony and, 140–142; Cavell on, 146–155; Austin on, 152–154; Fish on, 155–159
Origen, 33–34
Ortega y Gasset, Jose, 190–191
Ovid, 30

Paradise Lost (Milton), 50, 76
Paul, St., 35–36, 51, 204
Peirce, C. S., 48, 113–114
Pelicans, history of allusion to, 43–48
Personification, 165–166, 181; contrasted with metaphor 6–7
Pliny the Elder, 30
Poetics (Aristotle), 59–60, 61–63, 73, 98–99, 199
Pound, Ezra, 102–106
Propertius, 30
Prosopopeia, 175–181
Proust, Marcel, 132, 137, 170–173

Quintilian, 30–31, 130–131, 182; on synecdoche, 133–134; on irony, 137

Ransom, John Crowe, 186–187
Riffaterre, Michael, 175–177
Rimbaud, 100–101
Ratzinger, Joseph, 34–35
Resemblance: as factor in metaphor, 61–68; as a factor in simile, 123–128. *See also* Simile
Rhetoric (Aristotle), 59, 63, 80, 199
Richard II (Shakespeare), 44–45, 75, 79–80
Richards, I. A., 1, 52, 85, 86, 93, 94–95, 115
Ricoeur, Paul, 48, 65, 66, 173
Rousseau, Jean-Jacques, 121–122

Saward, Fr. John, 26–27, 28
Schlegel, A. W., 64
Scientific language and metaphor, 159–160
Seidel, Frederick, 116–117
Shakespeare, William, 3, 4, 8, 44–45, 56, 68–69, 75, 79–80, 81, 85, 86–87, 95–96, 125, 137, 140–141, 150, 167
Shelley, Percy, 128, 195, 204
Silk, Michael, 72–73
Simile, 11, 74–75, 125; distinct from metaphor, 53–54, 80–82, 200–201; epic similes, 75–77, 79; "like" contrasted with "as," 105; and similarity, 123–128
Socrates, 49
Steiner, George, 108
Stern, Gustav, 52
Stevens, Wallace, 49, 57, 168–169, 185–186, 188–190, 191, 197–200, 205–206; "The Motive for Metaphor," 191–197; bizarre examples of metaphor from, 201–204
Synechdoche: Vico on, 90; contrasted with metonymy, 130–131, 134, 167

Tempest, The (Shakespeare), 137
Tenor, 1–2, 8, 32, 33–34, 52–53, 84–87, 91
Terence, 29

Tertullian, 31–33, 51
Theological implications of metaphor, 21–29, 31–40
Tolstoy, Leo, 129–130
Trope: contrasted with figure, 31
Twelfth Night (Shakespeare), 150

Varro, 29–30
Vehicle, 1–2, 8, 32, 33–34, 52–53, 84–87, 91
Vendler, Helen, 108–109
Verisimilitude: metonymy and, 73
Vickers, Brian, 131–132, 167

Vico, 87–91; on metaphor, 89, 122–123; on metonymy, 90, 122–123; on synecdoche, 90, 122–123; on irony, 90, 122–123; on origins of language, 121

Wielockx, Robert, 25–26
Winter's Tale, The (Shakespeare), 68–69
Worstward Ho (Beckett), 69–70

Yeats, W. B. (William Butler), 45, 115, 183